THE CRAFT
OF TV COPYWRITING

Other Allison & Busby "Writer's Guides"

Writers' Questions Answered by Gordon Wells

The Craft of Writing Articles by Gordon Wells

The Magazine Writer's Handbook by Gordon Wells

The Craft of Novel-Writing by Dianne Doubtfire

How to Write Stories for Magazines by Donna Baker

The Craft of Writing Romance by Jean Saunders

How to Publish Yourself by Peter Finch

How to Publish Your Poetry by Peter Finch

How to Write for Children by Tessa Krailing

An Allison & Busby book
Published in 1988 by
W.H. Allen & Co. Plc
44 Hill Street
London W1X 8LB

Printed and bound in Great Britain by
Anchor Brendon Ltd., Tiptree, Essex

ISBN 0 85031 930 7

Contents

First Words

1. **Good Ideas Don't Care Who They Come To**   9

   The way in. What the professionals forget.
   Look for the fourth idea. Remember when....
   Make your commercial welcome. Creating a
   favourable climate for choice. Dancing girls. A
   time for humour. Be self-indulgent. Using your
   experience. What kind of writer? Knowing what
   is real.

2. **Getting Ideas**   21

   Where do I start. Refreshes the parts....
   Different kinds of ideas. I'm thinking. Involve
   yourself. Getting ideas from ideas. Giving you
   ideas.... Still more ideas....

3. **Ideas: Putting Them Down and Putting Them Up**   33

   The accepted way. The other way. Is it worth
   presenting?

4. **The Magic Shape**   41

   Structuring a TV commercial. It's simple but
   not easy. The big O. Striking a chord. The
   music of persuasion. Variations on a theme. Be
   honest with yourself.

5. **How to Win an Award**   53
   I'll buy that.

6. Great Commercial   57

"Wish I'd thought of that!" The third
ingredient. Stay a consumer.

7. Research: Who Needs It?   65

What is research? What research measures.
Who conducts the research. Preparing for
research. The scenario.

8. Making Your Commercial   75

The role of the writer. The production
company. Choosing a production company.
Choosing a director. The pre-production
meeting. Sir! The editor. The words... and
music. Can you trust your director? End shot.

9. Selling Yourself   91

Getting ahead of the game. Getting a reel.
Getting an interview. Your first interview. What
are my chances?

10. Planning Your Career   99

Stay a writer always. Career or job sequence?

Last Word   105

Glossary of Terms   107

Bibliography   117

College courses in Advertising   119

Recruitment Agencies   121

Index   123

First Words

While the rest of British business was basking in the golden years of the late 1960s and early 1970s, the advertising industry was having its recession.

An industry with a total person-power of 25,000 shrank to 17,000 in a matter of months. This was not entirely unexpected. Advertising had been fattening since the late 1950s and oedema had set in badly with the bonanza of commercial television.

By the mid 1970s, however, it had become lean and it has stayed that way. It was this leanness which saved it from the common industrial disaster and indeed which helped it prosper while other industries declined over the following fifteen years.

The result of all this was a considerably reduced intake of young people over this period. Traditionally thought of as a young industry, advertising became an ageing one. And the agencies slowly began to think about rectifying this.

All this is relevant to you, the reader of this book. It means that there is a real opportunity, though still not an easy one, for new recruits, particularly recruits with a better than average knowledge of the craft of writing TV advertising – that still-booming, nickel-plated shareholding which resists all the promotions and deals of the competitive but passive media of magazine, newspaper, and poster.

TV is not passive. It comes at you. It forces its attention upon you. The programmes and commercials alike are hypnotic.

One can understand the fascination of the programmes, but it is the fascination of the TV commercial that mystifies; the viewer may lose patience with the programme, but very rarely does he or she feel impatient enough with a commercial to switch off or over to another channel.

Like some little works of cine-art, the TV commercial appears and the viewer is prepared to sit and watch again and again in silence, sometimes with the approach of a smile on the lips.

On the other hand, the commercial appears and you can't hear what it says for the catcalls of derision from the watching viewers. Haven't you ever sat there, sneering at the unnaturalness of what happens in that natural break? The lack of any sense of reality? The patronising reproduction of what someone thinks is the way you live and behave?

Of course, you have. And you can do better than that, can't you? You've said it often enough. And, of course, you can!

If you really want to do it for a good living, really want to, this book will be invaluable to you as a guide to what some consider to be the most important aspect of creative advertising. At interviews, the question most frequently asked of the young writer or art director is: "Have you done any television?" Yet, in terms of any kind of training or instruction, the craft of writing TV commercials is the most neglected. Although it is not the only creative skill that will be required of you as an advertising *creative**, it is clearly thought by employers to be a specific craft skill. To my knowledge, this is the first book to deal with it specifically.

*For explanation of this and other words italicized in the text, see Glossary, p. 107.

1
Good Ideas Don't Care Who They Come To

The advertising agency business is short on people who know how to write a TV commercial of the kind the viewer instinctively likes and reacts to. So there's plenty of room for people who can. People like you, for example. Someone who likes dealing in words and ideas, who likes to write, someone who has learned how to shape a commercial, to structure it in the way that is rewarding to the eye and the ear, satisfying to the needs of the consumer, and effective for the advertiser.

Writing ability is, of course, important and can be learned and improved by practice; what is more important, however, is that you – the student, the beginner – are still close to the consumer and his or her world; you are an "outsider" – and that puts you ahead of the game.

With your virgin mind, your direct approach to life unhampered by the affectation of technique, and with your personal, first-hand, consumer's knowledge of what makes a good or a bad commercial, you can't help but be ahead of the "insider", ahead of those already in the game. You are equipped with that unclouded insight that is needed to write the kind of commercials that contain none of the false human premises that make you cringe, that make your toes curl whenever they appear on your TV screen.

The way in

The opportunities are there, so how do you get in?

There is no recognized way in to the job of writing TV

commercials. Apart from a few outstanding Colleges of Further Education (see p. 118), there is no significant industry-organised system of learning the business. It is an open competition. Anyone can try. And anyone who has shown an interest, which you clearly have, can succeed.

Ask around in the advertising business and you'll find that few people wanted to be an advertising man or woman from the age of 5. 80% got into the business by happenstance or were led there by a careers advisor who really didn't think they'd make good teachers. For creative people I'd say the happenstance-rate is higher. So if you found this book through idle browsing in a bookshop, you'll be no exception. You're one of the accidents that happen to advertising.

What the professionals forget

What I am really trying to get across to you is this: you don't have to be scared of the so-called professionals. In the main, that is their problem: they are too professional. They have forgotten one important thing – how to view like a consumer.

You need to know at this point that it is the *creative department* of an advertising agency, staffed by ordinary, averagely intelligent people who write the commercials. These are the creatives. (They also write the *press ads* and the *brochures, posters*, and *radio commercials* – skills you will need to acquire but are not discussed here; enough books have been written about them already – see Bibliography, p. 117).

These creatives, I repeat, are ordinary, averagely intelligent people. I describe them in this way so that you will no longer hold them in awe. Some are impressive. Some get good ideas, certainly. But no more and no better than you can get if you apply yourself honestly and assiduously.

So if you are worried about getting good ideas – don't. You'll get plenty of bad ones – who doesn't? – but if you go on looking hard enough, the good ones will come to you, too.

Look for the fourth idea

It may be invented, but there is a little story told by the *creative director* of one of our most famous advertising agencies. When asked what was the secret of his agency's creative success, he answered: "Our first ideas are no better than anyone else's. Neither are our second. Nor our third. But the difference between us and other agencies is, we go on to look for the fourth idea; others stop at the third."

I say again: good ideas don't care who they come to. They just seem to come to those who know where to look for them, those who look for them harder and sometimes longer.

I'll tell you later where to look, how to look, and what to do with your ideas when they arrive. How long you look, how hard, depends on you.

The *client* even has a good idea sometimes. Or the seeds of one, at least. And so do those people in suits called *account executives*, the so-called business men of the agency, traditionally and wilfully dismissed by creatives as being non-creative. Account execs aren't supposed ever to have an idea, nor the ability to recognise one when it's put under their noses.

But good ideas don't care who they come to. Really. It's just that some people get them more often than others because they know where ideas come from and how to recognise them and what to do with them. I repeat this because I am anxious to make you believe it so that you will not be frightened of the people who are doing what you want to do better.

Good ideas will come to you as often as they come to anyone else – more often, if you apply yourself to the problem of selling the product in a way that *you*, the consumer, know is the way that will make *you*, the consumer, buy.

Remember when ...

In other words: don't lose your advantage by trying to become an advertising creative too soon. Stay a consumer all your advertising life. Never forget what your reactions are to the commercials you watch now. Remember and learn from your reactions and experience as a consumer and use it when you start writing your commercials.

Be a professional in your approach, become a craftsman in your work, but stay a consumer at heart.

The good advertising man remembers what it was like before he was an advertising man. If I had to select one attribute of a good TV writer of commercials, it would be this one, this most powerful of all abilities: to be able to remember when. All the great Hollywood moguls had it. Rich they may have become, but they never forgot where they came from and what it was like back there...

I put this ability at the top of the list because the main function of the TV commercial writer is to act as a go-between for the consumer and the advertiser. He is an interpreter of the product. He must represent the product in a way that makes it welcome. He cannot behave like an old-fashioned face-to-face, foot-in-the-door salesman. (How would you like six of them knocking on your door, selling up to six different products not just once every hour, but four times, just when you were settling down to look at your favourite TV programme?)

Make your commercial welcome

TV advertising should not intrude. It should be welcome. This is particularly necessary for TV advertising because it is by its nature an active medium; it produces more powerful responses from the consumer, for or against the advertiser and his product. The more unwelcome the commercial, the greater the antipathy when a buying decision involving choice has to be made.

Only the staple, monopolistic product can afford to ignore this point of view, and even then not for very long. There's always an alternative being conceived in some test tube, or a consumer association somewhere just around the corner. And failing that, there's a growing number of remote controls in the hands of the viewers!

Much of TV advertising is unwelcome because it is untimely. This is a problem that must be and can be overcome. A way must be found to penetrate the minds of the *target audience* at times when that audience is not immediately interested – and yet the commercial must still contain all the information that is needed by those who are interested at that time.

Consequently the commercial must be acceptable at all times and be of such a nature that it generates a build-up of goodwill against the time when the uninterested target audience becomes actively interested.

Creating a favourable climate for choice

Few advertisers understand this. It is natural that they should expect the whole of the outside world to be as immediately interested as they are in their product; but the fact is that the whole world isn't, not all together, not all at the same time, and sometimes they won't ever be if the advertising has anything to do with it.

Good advertising people – particularly on the creative side – are instinctively aware of this, and know that their commercials must represent an investment fund of present goodwill in order to secure future interest and preference. Ronnie Kirkwood of The Kirkwood Company phrased this as "creating a favourable climate of choice". This only ceases to be important if the client deals from an upturned plastic milk-crate in Oxford Street.

Creating a favourable climate of choice means building up a favourable attitude, while conveying information of one kind or another, against the time when the uninterested consumer is faced with making a buying decision.

Dancing girls

The creative person appreciates this need to write a commercial the viewer will want to watch again and again. One research firm, Eric

Clucas & Associates, measures this quality as "entertainment value". This doesn't mean dancing girls and a swinging music track or pop-promo video-effects. It means that the commercial will have some kind of real value which the consumer can relate to, a value that makes it a commercial she or he will watch with a sense of reward or satisfaction, a commercial that contributes to his or her life in some small way and will lead to the appreciation of the product or the advertiser.

The good creative writer somehow understands this instinctively because he or she is more of a consumer than a manufacturer. This, indeed, is the creative person's strength and reason for living.

He is a consumer writing commercials for other consumers.

So, it is clear that the commercial must delight the viewer in some way or other, at whatever point in the buying-interest curve the commercial is seen.

A time for humour

Suspicion tends to condemn the commercial that sets out to have this quality of delight, particularly if the delight is based upon humour.

Winston Fletcher in his book, *Meetings, Meetings*, quotes Claude Hopkins, an advertising man of the 1930s depression period. Hopkins was of the opinion that people wouldn't buy anything from a clown. It was his attack upon humour in commercials and was, I suppose, based upon the grim realities of life at that time.

It is an attitude that has been shown to have outlasted its validity. Yet clients still tend to suspect commercials that delight the consumer. The idea of "entertainment value" is one that Eric Clucas has a hard time explaining away.

It is not surprising then that funny commercials are frowned upon by clients who wear grey flannel faces and rictal smiles.

Yet it doesn't worry you, the consumer, does it? Does it worry you, for example, that those famous, funny Sony commercials were all about a tiny (Japanese, get it?) cult product that was made with such integrity that it could survive the exasperated contempt poured on it by another, contrasting cult figure – John Cleese, very tall and equally full of integrity. Weren't they enjoyable, and didn't they make you think well of the product?

Unfortunately, such qualities of watchability are often described as self-indulgent, uncommercial in the business sense, and too "creative".

Be self-indulgent

Self-indulgent it may very well be, yet this need not be wrong. My definition of a creative writer is: a sensitive and intuitive go-between for the manufacturer and the consumer. It applies here.

If a commercial pleases the creative writer then it should be because the writer is pleasing the consumer inside himself. And that's what you are at this moment: a consumer. And you know what pleases and persuades the likes of you.

This quality of self-delight, of course, is open to abuse and misuse, and this is where everything can go wrong. Normally it goes wrong when the film-maker in the writer, the creative inside the creative, takes over; when the technician becomes more involved in technique than in the product and its consumer. Then the delight is self-orientated, technical, insensitive, and wrong.

Choose your parents carefully

Because you are a consumer and because you will stay that way, you won't make the mistakes I've been talking about. Unlike the time-patinated professional, you will remain sensitive to the consumer's real life. You will also go on watching television, the way you always have. The chances are you watch it more than most, because the chances are that you are in what the socio-demographers call the C^1C^2 bracket. What used to be called upper and lower working class. The more TV you watch, the more C^1C^2

you are. And that is definitely OK for a TV copywriter. It's OK because that's what all the really good TV commercial writers are (until they become over-educated in the business of writing TV commercials and infected by the AB mores forced upon them by their salary cheques.)

The advantage of being born in the C^1C^2 classification is more apparent in the work of writers of TV commercials than perhaps in any other area of money-making, except perhaps the pop world and in big bang wheeler-dealing. For one agency, it has become a very successful total image!

However: you have this priceless head-start of being brought up at your mother's knee. Few C^1C^2 children ever get packed off to public school, so their view of real life is rarely distorted by being incarcerated in some anachronistic prism.

You chose your parents carefully, then, and you are what you are (and proud of it, I suppose, because you can't think of anything else to be) and you are primed by all your experiences to start writing TV commercials for the people you are going to leave behind....

You are superbly equipped to talk to the people through the medium of the TV commercial because you are one of the people who know all about what the kids will eat, what your mate will swallow, and when and how and why; what it costs in money and grey hairs to keep a family going, your ego boosted, and your marriage as alive as the cartoon marriage of *George and Lynn*; and what it takes out of a weekly wage packet to prove that your pulling power is as great as any Strongbow archer.

Using your experience

You have experienced it all, one way or another. Constipation. Headaches. Dinner at a country house with a charming French man at your side, or a low-cut lady opposite – an everyday TV experience in our everyday fantasy of the luxury things in life. And you've eaten Kentucky Fried on your lap, savouring the secret recipe of Colonel Sanders, while you watch and see revealed the less than secret recipe for a lusty life doled out by ITV and BBC soaps.

There you are, then. In your armchair, watching. You are one of the people who keep TV alive. Why shouldn't it keep you alive? You're one of the people who buys the goodies that TV tells you about. Who better, then, to do the selling than you?

Education? Don't let it worry you, even if you have had one. Being born into a TV-watching family is better qualification than any degree when it comes to writing real-life TV commercials. Hang on to the head-start your father and mother gave you. It is a valuable inheritance that could put more than one silver spoon on your table.

If your kitchen table at home was deal, hang on to that too; when you become successful, it will go very nicely in the garden-floor, imitation country-style kitchen of your period house in Blackheath/ Highgate/Solihull/Calderstones/Cheadle Hulme.

What kind of writer?

Before we get into the writing of TV commercials, I want you to stop and think.

What kind of a TV commercial writer do you want to be?

A star, of course. But that comes a little later. For now, think about the kind of commercials you want to write and I'll give you some clue as to whether or not you'll succeed.

In the TV advertising business, there are lots of different kinds of writers, but they fall mainly into three categories.

First of all, there's the "old" kind. This kind is made up of the people who pride themselves on their technical competence. Their knowledge of the rules. The things that have worked in the past. The exact number of words that the average fast *pitchman* can say in 30 seconds. Usually, but not always, this kind produces commercials full of amazed housewives and whiter than white washing. Or bellowing talking heads. Or crass demonstrations that prove nothing. (A distressing thing is, some young writers are quite happy to write this kind of commercial; it's got nothing to do with age, just their upbringing.)

This is the kind of writer you don't really want to be. Which

17

means, this is the kind of agency you don't want to write for if you believe, as I do, that even TV commercials have a social responsibility not to diminish the quality of our lives. This kind of writer has forgotten what it was like to be a consumer; more likely, their attitudes towards advertising were formed long before TV commercials were invented! Or they have inherited through their social genes the same contempt for the consumer that made young sub-editors write jingoistic World War Two headlines at the time of the Falklands affair.

The second kind tends to be the younger kind. Experienced but untouched by his experience, this writer still thinks that the latest visual technique, with as little "chat" as possible, is the way TV commercials should be made. Left alone, this kind would write any agency out of business.

They would never admit – they would rather deny – ever having been consumers of the kind that actually watch the telly, perhaps because they never were or because they despise the consumer and themselves for doing so.

Then there's the third kind. They come in all ages. These are the writers who have decided, as I want you to decide, that the kind of commercial they want to write is the kind that talks to the consumer as they would like to be talked to themselves.

They don't underestimate the consumer, nor do they over-estimate him. They get it just right. Because they know. Probably because they remember what it was like being a consumer before they became advertising writers.

The commercials they have set out to be good at writing are those that seem real to them. Not the ones that amazed with their cleverness, but the commercials that struck some kind of chord of recognition. Touched some reality.

Knowing what is real

By real, I don't necessarily mean factual, or sober. Funny can be real. Fantasy can be real if it is a reflection of the consumer's fantasy. Romance can be real when it is done with insight and an understanding of the need we all have for the ideal and the only-imaginable. And satire can be real, if the satire is something we can all share, not just an in-joke played out around some obscure reference that does nothing more than show how esoteric the writer's experience is.

Summary

* *Don't let the professionals frighten you. Everyone was a beginner once.*

* *Good ideas don't care who they come to – but they seem to come most often to those who look for them longest and hardest.*

* *Sit down and write your own impressions of the TV commercial scene now – while you are still a consumer – and keep it for future reference.*

* *Decide what kind of TV copywriter you are going to be.*

* *Do both the above – before you go any further.*

2

Getting Ideas

"Where do I start?"

What is an "idea"? Where do you go to get one? How do you know what to look for? How do you do it every time? *"Where do I start?"*

These questions, in various forms, are the questions I've had asked me countless times by beginners, sometimes by awe-stricken book-keepers I've met at PTA meetings, or at parties, but mostly by students I've taught on advertising courses. And the most panic-stricken voices of them all came from the last.

So just to quell the panic momentarily, I'm going to repeat what I said in the last chapter: *good ideas don't care who they come to.*

The trick is recognizing them when they do appear. Eventually you'll learn to do this instinctively. You'll just know a good idea when it comes. You'll be certain about it when someone says, "That's just what I was going to say."

You won't have to ask if it's a good idea. You'll know. And knowing, like creativity, comes from hard practice. Tony Brignull, one of the very top writers in the advertising business, tells the story of his learning to play the cello. For the first six months he had to ring up his cello teacher every time he wanted to practise. He had to play the A string over the phone, just to make sure he had it properly tuned. Gradually, from practice, he began to hear it for himself, he began to know without asking.

Refreshes the parts...

Let's try to define a good idea, just so that we can pin it down quickly before it flits by.

An idea, of course, is a creative thought, and a creative thought is what it says it is: a thought that creates something that didn't exist before. It may be, but rarely is, something entirely new – like creating the Universe.

Or it may be a new way of perceiving something as old as creation.

Or a new way of putting together two or more existing thoughts.

Or a new way of expressing something that's been said a thousand times before, but doing it in such a way that it has new values.

Whatever of these things it is, it will have a thrilling magic about it that will make others feel that they are witnessing something never seen before. Or, better still, becoming aware of something that they may have looked at a thousand times but never really seen.

Isn't this the reason why creativity is so essential to human life? Isn't this the best argument for the creative arts? The fact that they constantly refresh, have the ability to reawaken our wonder at life, and make it continually worth living?

Now that's all very well and rarified. So, back to earth. What you have to do is to turn the process of getting ideas into a repeatable, business-like process, to make it commercial – in both senses of the word. Programme yourself so that you have a set way of going about it, so you don't have to ring up your cello-teacher each time. So that it becomes instinctive.

Different kinds of ideas

Now we know what an idea is, what has it got to do with writing TV commercials?

This:

An idea is a vehicle for presenting the product in such a way that the product gains for itself the right to be part of the consumer's life.

Every product has a right to exist. It has a reason for living; there's a reason why it continues to turn up on your shelves. Your job is to make sure it continues to turn up there, continues to live and grow.

Your job is to grasp hold of an idea that presents the product for the umpteenth time in such a way that it refreshes the consumer's interest in it, and desire for it, and makes them consider it in a new and appealing light.

Where will these ideas come from?

There are three sources of ideas.

In the product From a long-term business point of view, the best ideas come from within the product – the way it's made, what it's made from, who makes it; ideas just waiting for you to seek them out. Sometimes they are painfully obvious. Like the amazing, new, secret ingredient, for example; so obvious that your client may feel that to shout about it is all you need to do. You don't need an idea.

Well, shouting isn't what you need to do, and you do need an idea to establish the relevance of that secret ingredient.

Sometimes ideas are less obvious and need searching out, and these are the ones that usually make the best ads. They may even need actual experience of the product, or a trip to the factory where you'll rediscover what no-one sees anymore: a process, for example, a way they go about things that may be undramatic in itself but is a perfect and convincing expression of the basic idea of the product.

The Volkswagen team of 15 inspectors descending on every single car.

The engineer at Rolls Royce worried that you can actually hear the clock ticking when you're driving along.

The marrow-bone jelly in the can of dog-food.

A unit trust as full of integrity and financial nous as the Quaker family that created it, evidenced by their decision to invest only in those companies that have a concern for our quality of life.

There are the aspects of the product that are built-in, have always been there, but have remained unnoticed until you came along, with your fresh outsider's eye, and saw them for what they were.

23

And there you have it – the beginning of an idea!

Around the product Sometimes, of course, there really will be nothing in the product that can be used to capture interest. Don't let it worry you. Look again, just a little harder, don't take someone else's word that what you're looking for isn't there; but then when you finally have to give up, what you do is you look around the product.

What's it doing in the world? Where has it been? Who is using it? How are they using it? Is there a new way to use it? What do people say about it? In other words, don't think about what it is; think about what it does. Think of it as a person. Imagine someone who, for all you know, hasn't a single distinguishing feature. This person is full of all the acceptable virtues, but is nothing special – except to family and friends.

Or so you thought. Until you discover that she's just spent a whole year on a desert island living with a man she met through a classified ad.

Suddenly this product takes on a whole new life, a new image, a new interest. It's not what it's made of, it's what it has made of itself!

So look around the product. And if there's still nothing that would make you want it with you on a desert island, go to the third and often the most rewarding source of ideas.

Outside the product I wrote earlier about the commercial as a vehicle for positioning the product as a part of the consumer's life.

Here, I am going to write about the commercial as a vehicle for making the consumer's life part of the product.

Out there beyond the covers of this book, it's all happening. Life goes on. Except, perhaps, for the poor TV copywriter who has rifled through two important sources of ideas and come up with nothing.

The product has nothing going for it except its basic integrity of purpose and performance.

That's when the writer starts to look outside the product for an idea, a vehicle for presenting the product in a way that gives it new interest, new appeal.

24

The writer starts to look at life. What's happening out there that is relevant to my product? What has happened in my life that is relevant? What is going to happen that might shine a new light from a new angle, that could be used to throw an interesting new pattern of light and shade upon my problem?

What part of life can I lay claim to, stake out and use and talk about in such a way that it becomes irrevocably the territory of my product?

What do I have in that great big plastic dustbin liner I call my experience of life – what is there in it I can drag out and use to dramatize the worth of my product?

I'm thinking

I have this Iron Supplement Capsule to write about. It's a good product, useful when needed. But so are many other iron capsule products. But there is a special ingredient, a piece of information, an angle, a story into which I can inextricably weave my product.

There is this little bit of information I picked up from somewhere long ago; it's to do with anaemia. Our grandmothers rarely suffered from it. Not because they ate more greens. But because they cooked them in iron saucepans. And what do we use today? Aluminium. Stainless steel. Glass-lined. Earthenware. They don't rust overnight... so they don't provide that extra daily dose of iron that could make all the dietary difference, especially in a doubtful 1980s fast-food diet.

And there I have an idea. A basis for conviction. A credible context in which my story – about the gradual breakdown of the capsule in the stomach and gradual absorption into the blood – somehow becomes more credible, more worth looking into.

And it came from an odd piece of information I picked up on the way from a manual on nutrition and stuffed into my big black plastic bag. Every writer needs a bag like this. Start filling yours now.

Involve yourself

"Where do I start?" you ask. At any one of three sources listed above. All you have to bring to the process is your own personality, your own individuality – perhaps the most important special ingredient that a writer will ever find. Your own way of looking at things, your own experience, the contents of your bag – these are the things that will inform and distinguish your writing in a way that nothing else will. It's the difference that makes some people famous and others not so famous. And out of it comes your own way of "talking", your own style, your own way of making your ideas work as a commercial.

Getting ideas from ideas

Thinking is the initial creative act. Writing it down is also creative; indeed, the very act of thinking or writing is itself an idea-creating act. So start thinking if you want to think, start writing if you want to write. Creating creates creativity.

One of the ways to start thinking is to look at what other people have thought. That's not cheating. Everything comes from something – except that original act of creation. Some of the best commercials are adaptations of old techniques, new representations of old ideas. In fact, one of the best ways to start yourself thinking of ideas is to look at the ways in which other people have executed their ideas.

There are as many ways of executing ideas for commercials as there are filmic formats. It is taken as understood that you are reading this book because you are interested in communication. Of all the forms of the media, you are particularly interested in the visual arts, the moving image, the graphic presentation. It can, therefore, be taken for granted that you are a watcher of films and television, a looker at pictures and sculpture.

This also being the case, you will know – perhaps without knowing it – that you have experience of the basic ways of making ideas work in commercial form. But let's go through them, because knowing what kinds of commercial you *can* make can give you ideas for the commercial you *could* make. A technique, a piece of camera work, an actor, a cartoon character – any one of them could supply just that extra little piece of inspiration, that extra connection between half-connected ideas that can make an idea just burst into life.

TV copywriters will admit that getting in a reel of specimen films from a *TV production company* can make quite a difference to their day! Viewing good commercials can lift their minds out of a rut, give them a new angle, help them think of a fresh possibility.

Giving you ideas...

Drama-real This is the form that is based upon the human-interest story-line; in the business it is usually condemned by being called *slice of life*. Here we are not talking about slice of life, but about drama-real.

Unlike the slice of life format, the drama-real has as its distinguishing feature people you can believe in! Real characterisation, believable settings, and situations that reflect real life.

Some drama-real commercials are a triumph. The cast is accurate, precise. The dialogue is natural and characterful. The relationship between the people is full of dramatic tension. And the commercials are "shot" with all the craft that has made the British Film Industry famous.

Mini-dramas, played around a tiny fragment of life, but nevertheless accurate observations precisely made and usually so closely in touch with reality that they have a disconcerting but persuasive effect.

It is a delight to say that there are many of them on view at the time of writing.

The Cointreau couple (probably lovers by the time of publishing) are literally a perennial example. The first film ever made ran for four consecutive years around about Christmas time. Romantic it is, but very real in the romantic tradition. And the relationship between a Frenchman, warm, romantic, confident, but not

27

arrogant, and an English woman, cool but quietly thrilled, develops nicely from commercial to commercial. And what's very much to the point, they are established as metaphors for Cointreau and for the ice you take with it.

In the world of finance, the Apple commercials stand out as a moment of flint-edged time in the City death struggle, the characters representing not the old and young generation, but the fourth and fifth generation of computers!

And the Midland Bank Vector commercial, again a beautifully cast, acted, and directed moment when the human individual begins to gain ascendancy over the faceless financiers, thanks to the bank that listens to what human beings say.

Three examples of dramatic values being used to position a product credibly and appealingly in the life of the potential consumer.

Drama-doc There are two kinds: demonstration commercials and testimonial commercials; they happen separately and together.

Once upon a time a demonstration commercial was usually *in-studio* with very simple, often stilted, and often puzzling demonstrations of arcane aspects of the product. But now the important feature of the product is demonstrated in dramatic and far more relevant ways.

Witness the Pilkington glass commercial with a well-known actor telling you entertainingly about the company, while the subplot of a man with a gun is built up; the dénouement comes when we realise that the actor has been talking to us from behind a huge sheet of glass which is invisible to us until a bullet smashes into it (but happily not through it!). A reflection of the times, perhaps, but nevertheless a vivid and convincing demonstration of the product's virtues.

Testimonial commercials also strive for the more dramatic presentation. No longer are they content simply to show a personality endorsing the product by its use. Now they go into show-biz with a well-known media personality "representing" the company and relating directly with the ordinary person in the street or, more usually, in the supermarket. This area is a favourite of the big soap companies. And they do try these days to relate more

28

closely to real-life. Washing-up liquid turns up in a combined testimonial/demonstration which takes place in a school dining room, for example. And high-ranking police officers stand on motorway bridges and tell us about safety tyres of a particular brand.

The drama-real commercial goes for all the values of the dramatic arts. The drama-doc goes for all the hype and hyperbole of show-biz, bringing it into people's lives by association with famous people. And that's what advertising is all about: bringing the product into people's lives in a way that makes them accept it, prefer it, choose it.

Surreal This is the kind of commercial that really does need a lot of "writing" and very little writing. And such commercials are very difficult, almost by definition, to describe. Mainly because it is the particular nature of the images that is important. The effects have to be seen. They are not only the kind of commercials that play around with perspective and relativity, but they often have indefinable frameworks of time and place. And their atmosphere is intensely personal to either the "writer" of the film or the Director. When they have this individual, personal quality, they are stunning. But too often they become sub-versions of Monty Python's Flying Circus. Or they become imitative of the fantasy film. When they are truly original, however, they set off a new style of their own and, with skill, make a segment of this particular genre the product's very own.

But not all surreal commercials are this successful.

Animation used to mean just cartoon. Now it means everything that involves everything that isn't "live action". Live action, for want of a better definition, is what you see when you are the camera, assuming that you have normal vision and aren't subject to hallucination!

Anything else is, broadly speaking, animation. *Stop motion, stepped frames, over-cranking, under-cranking*, they're all, technically speaking, animation. But the main use of the word is to describe the use of *artwork*, either handmade artwork or computer-based.

Cartoon, not surprisingly, is animation. We could have included this under surreal, but I chose to put it here because, unlike the surreal commercial style mentioned above, a cartoon can be very direct in its selling of the product, losing on the way its appeal as a cartoon perhaps, but exploiting all the delightful impossibilities of which the style is capable. I don't need to tell you how the cartoon technique can compress, emphasise, or speed up all or any part of the action in a way that, perhaps, live action can't. And, the greatest virtue of all, cartoon allows you to make extravagant filmic statements in order to make a point that would otherwise be totally rejected by the viewer in a live action film. If you've ever seen a cat flattened by a steam-roller then, a half-second later, spring back into vengeful life, you'll know what I mean.

Computer-based animation lends itself stunningly to the commercial that is dealing with the technological or the technocratic. It has also been used brilliantly by one electronics company to create a *spokesman* character for its audio products.

Artwork animation is a way of describing the commercials that are based upon either a succession of flat artwork images filmed on a *rostrum camera*, just the way Disney made Mickey Mouse, or the kind that is artwork drawn from and based directly upon previously shot *film footage*. The advantages here are of simplicity, selection, and a distinctive style. (Also, you don't have to pay repeats to the artist!) For example, if you want to throw emphasis on a very stylish lady, swinging her way down a street, men's heads turning as she passes by, first you shoot it on film. Then, as the basis for the artwork, you might select the lady, the men turning their heads, a lamp-post (or whatever indicates it's a street). Leave out all the rest – other unwanted passers-by, traffic, buildings – and you've made your point immediately and distinctively.

And finally, for the moment anyway, there's the *Puppet* animation – you could describe it as three-dimensional cartoon. The "puppets" can either be creatures, human or otherwise, or even products animated by stop-frame camerawork. A bar of chocolate can "make" itself. A tin of cocoa can self-determine itself from the bottom up. Cartons of yoghurt can behave like the beautiful people, skiing at St Moritz, or kicking sand into a tub of a rival brand. All before your very eyes, and seemingly without human assistance. A lot of fun, keeps the kids amused for hours – well, thirty seconds anyway.

Still more ideas...

Later on you will read about research; not too much, but enough to make this marketing tool valuable to you. The point of raising it here is: research can be yet another important source of ideas.

There are basically two kinds of research. *Product research:* that is, what people think of the product, how they'd like it changed or improved, how they use it, new ways they think they might like to use it, and so on. This kind of information can be a goldmine, especially if your product has become bedded down in the past, seems old-fashioned, needs bringing up to date, or has reached a plateau in sales.

Usually this kind of research is undertaken by *group discussion.* This is your chance to meet the people you have to write for. The real, living, breathing, awkward consumer. Just one word of advice when you go to a group discussion: don't let any of the group know that you write the commercials; it can get very upsetting for you if you do! Stay anonymous and with a bit of luck you'll hear something that sets off a thought, that leads to another thought, that could lead on to the big idea you need.

The other kind of research is *consumer research,* which is a fascinating investigation into the life-styles of people in general, not just your potential customers. The things you learn about the way people live! Makes you want to go away and write the great consumer novel. And what a storehouse of insights consumer research can be: out of it comes knowledge of the consumer which you can put together with your knowledge of the product and with your sense of drama and your knowledge of how ideas can be communicated – and the ideas will be falling over themselves to get on to the studio floor!

31

Summary

*   *Look for ideas: in the product, around the product, outside the product.*

*   *Never throw anything away – it could be useful.*

*   *To start you thinking, think of an execution.*

*   *Ideas create ideas create ideas.*

*   *Keep in touch with your market.*

*   *Listen to your audience.*

3

Ideas: Putting Them Down and Putting Them Up

By now, of course, you will have read this chapter heading and realised it's about ways of putting your ideas down on paper and preparing them for *presentation*. It may strike you as odd that this stage comes before learning how to structure the commercial.

It may seem odd, but it isn't. You see, there are two ways of putting your idea into words and pictures.

First, there is the accepted way: a way that can be stultifying, sometimes paralysing, for those who are new to the game. And yet it is a way that is adhered to through thick and thin, simply, I think, because the TV copywriter is writing for others who are lazy, set in their ways or lacking in understanding of the medium of film.

This accepted way you must know about. But that's no reason why you shouldn't, for your own use, learn about the second way, a way that takes a little of the fear out of the somewhat rigorous and peculiar craft of structuring a thirty-, forty-, or sixty-second commercial.

The accepted way

The script and/or storyboard Writing a film of any kind requires that the writer describes a piece of action and sound in such a way that what is in his mind is conveyed to the other person.

Film is action and sound happening together in a relationship. It is a moving, flowing sequence, and it is this flow that is difficult and important to maintain within the short time-span of a commercial. (You'll soon discover that the fewer the cuts in a commercial, the longer it seems.)

The accepted way of putting an idea down on paper is by way of a *script* or a *scripted storyboard*.

A script has a description of the visual action written (usually) on the left-hand side of the piece of paper, complete with now almost laughable abbreviations, all of which are a hangover from the days when making a commercial had to have about it the protective mysteries of the cinematic craft.

On the right-hand side of the script, you'll see written down what you hear: speech, *sound effects*, music.

The whole script is regimented into separate and sometimes arbitrary paragraphs, and they are numbered!

This division is a symptom of the crass belief that a commercial is made up of pictures (supposedly the province of the art director only) and words (the domain of the copywriter), when in fact a film is a unified event, taking place at one time before your very eyes and ears.

The storyboard takes the idiocy of it one stage further.

The art director draws out a series of *frames* according to the number of numbered paragraphs. And under each frame he writes however many words the space will allow.

However big and beautiful the finished result is – and sometimes they are enormous things of stunning beauty; I've actually seen one so long that the man holding one end had to open the door of the meeting room and step out into the corridor so that the final pack shot frame could be revealed to the meeting – this convention of separated picture and sound is nothing more than an idiot board.

It is insulting to clients, who clearly are thought to be optically schizoid. If a client wants to be quite sure of the colour of the hair of the actors, their height, their ethnic origin, or their chest size, then there's a time and place for that: it's called the *pre-production meeting*.

The other way

The Scenario From what you have read earlier you will know that you don't need to be a writer to write a TV commercial.

You don't even have to know how to spell. Art directors write commercials as often as copywriters write commercials. And they do it simply by describing their idea in such a way that the film they see running in their head is transferred to the mind's eye of the other person. That's all.

And how do you do this? You write a *scenario*.

A scenario is quite simply a description of what you see in your mind's eye as if you were seeing it on the screen of your television set.

Below this paragraph there is the outline of a television screen. Look at it and imagine happening within that frame any commercial you happen to remember. Do it now, as an exercise in visual honesty: imagine a commercial you like and imagine it happening there on this screen.

What you imagined happening right there, that is if you did it honestly, was the commercial the way it happened shot by shot, just as it happened. You imagined nothing that could not appear on that screen. Now that's what you have to do when you describe your commercial in a scenario. You imagine it honestly. It takes a little practice, like most things do the first time you do them. But you soon get it. Your mind's eye will become a little private cinema, where everything *you* see can be seen by a camera.

Now, that commercial you saw happening on this page: describe what you saw – honestly and accurately. Do it as if you were telling a friend about it.

Don't get stilted. Stay casual and simple, without any more slang than is really relevant. Describe the action, say what you heard: words, sound effect, and music.

Tell it as if you were telling someone a story. Paint a picture with words.

If you want proof that it can be done, and that it works, just listen to "Book at Bedtime" on the radio. Just words – but the picture reception is amazing.

Is it worth presenting?

The scenario, then, is useful for two purposes: it helps you find out what kind of commercial you naturally incline towards writing; and it acts as a means of putting your idea down on paper *cinematically*.

Now we come to the third use of the scenario. The scenario is an effective method of selling your ideas.

The time will come when you have to present your work to a meeting – even if that meeting consists of just you and your creative director.

There are many ways of making such a presentation, almost as many as there are people who make them. You will have to find your way: the way that gets across your idea; the way that you find most comfortable and with which you feel confident. This is important: if you don't feel confident in yourself, then no one else can be expected to have confidence in you, no matter how good your commercial is. It's a sad fact of life, but there it is; many good ideas have come to nothing simply because they weren't presented well.

One thing is certain: unless you're very, very practised, the script and/or storyboard is the most difficult format to present from. The easiest way is with a scenario. And you just tell it as if you were telling the meeting a story, departing from the typed scenario, embellishing it spontaneously if you feel really confident to do so, but still using the scenario as something you can stay with, or depart from and go back to. You've prepared it beforehand; had it typed out; practised reading it aloud; even rehearsed a few ad libs.

So you feel totally at ease, completely in command of your material. Your confidence permeates your presentation, and spreads across the meeting. Take any applause – clients have been known to clap a good performance! – with fitting modesty.

But what if you are made to deal in script and/or storyboard? What you do then is have scripts and storyboard there and hand the scripts round if you must, but present from the scenario you've prepared as if you were reading from the script; and let the meeting work from the script. They'll soon give up and start to listen to you... telling them a story.

Summary

*   *The script and storyboard is static; film is fluid.*

*   *The scenario is fluid and cinematic.*

*   *Practise writing scenarios for three reasons:*

    1. Scenarios help you find out quickly what kind of commercials you will be good at writing.

    2. Scenarios help ideas come more fluently, make you think cinematically.

    3. Scenarios make presenting your ideas easier and more effective.

*   *Find out your presentation style and practise it.*

Allen Brady & Marsh Ltd.,
Lynton House,
7/12 Tavistock Square,
LONDON, W.C.1 H 9SX
Telephone: 01 388 1100

POST PRODUCTION SCRIPT

Client: MIDLAND BANK
Product: VECTOR
Job.No.: M2099T2417 87
Description:
Title: "LAUNCH REVISED TITLE" 1987
Producer:

Production Co.: SPOTS
Location: Studio
Transmission: 21.10.

70"
Date: 19th October

Peter Rich

SCENARIO

This commercial is a conversation between three people: the customer, the bank manager, the manager's assistant.

It take place in the manager's office.   There are blue and yellow touches in the office – pictures, vases and so on – to echo the Midland corporate colour scheme.

The principal action of the commercial is the conversation wherein the customer reverses the normal relationship by instructing the bank manager in what he, the customer, requires from his new bank account.

The bank manager is somewhat taken aback but is perfecly intelligent and able to cope.   His assistant is more of a plodding character who displays some nervousness, hesitation and indignation.   His principal lines are simply a disbelieving echo of the customer's demands (not scripted, see guide track.)

The Bank Manager accepts the customer's suggestions with some degree of controlled outrage, but because he is a capable and reasonable person he agrees to the somewhat surprising demands that the customer makes.   At the conclusion of the commercial we dissolve to end title.

SUPER: Vector logo
Midland Bank logo/ Midland
The Listening Bank.
Subject to status. Ring 01-200 0200 for written details.

A scenario is a description of the commercial in words. More often than not the scenario can create, as it does here, a more vivid picture in the mind than any number of storyboard frames. Agency: Allen Brady & Marsh Ltd. Creatives: Tony Wake, Paul Follett.

CUSTOMER: This is the listening bank, yes?

MANAGER: Yes, it is.

CUSTOMER: Good. I'd like a new kind of bank account.

MANAGER: (SURPRISED) A new kind of ...

CUSTOMER: ...bank account, yes. First if I write a cheque that's a little over my balance...

MANAGER: (LOOKS SLIGHTLY WORRIED. ASSISTANT ON THE OTHER HAND LOOKS POSITIVELY ALARMED) Yes....?

CUSTOMER: I6d like it <u>cashed</u>.

MANAGER: Cashed?

CUSTOMER: Yes... <u>cashed</u>...a free overdraft of two hundred and fifty pounds should do it.

MANAGER: Free overdraft!

ASSISTANT: Free overdraft!

CUSTOMER: And none of those acidic letters. Right?

MANAGER: Er...right.

CUSTOMER: (GOES ON REFLECTIVELY) I also want interest on my current account.

ASSISTANT: (INDIGNANTLY UNDER HIS BREATH) Interest on current account....! (ASSISTANT IS SCRIBBLING FURIOUSLY.)

CUSTOMER: ...and preferential consideration for larger overdrafts.

ASSISTANT: Preferential? (ASSISTANT LOOKS UP ENQUIRINGLY)

CUSTOMER: That's one "f".

ASSISTANT: ONE "f".

<u>VOICE OVER COMES IN AS WE CUT AWAY TO SHOW VECTOR BRANDING</u>

VO: There's now a new kind of bank account. For a new kind of customer. Vector from Midland.

CUSTOMER: Oh yes, and finally, no bank charges

(ASSISTANT BREAKS HIS PENCIL)

MANAGER: (AGHAST) No bank charges? But how can ewe make an honest profit?

CUSTOMER: I'll pay a simple, monthly fee....fixed in advance. Right?

(MANAGER SMILES THINLY)

MANAGER: Right.

CUSTOMER: Thanks for listening

MANAGER: (SMILING THROUGH GRITTED TEETH) Have a nice day

(THEY SHAKE HANDS. CUSTOMER LEAVES.)

VO: Vector from Midland. A new kind of bank account. For a new kind of customer.

4

The Magic Shape

Structuring a TV commercial

Now you know how to put down your ideas. You know how to go about deciding how you present them. And you have a way of coping with people who insist on seeing a script and storyboard. So now all you need is the commercial. You've got the medium. So now comes the message.

What I want you to do is to prove that writing a good commercial is much simpler than writing a bad one.

You do this in two stages.

First, I want you to try to describe a TV commercial you just can't bear watching! A commercial you loathe with passion. If you've got a tape recorder, use it. Tell it the way it is. Put it down on tape. If it helps you to get started, begin like this: "I saw a commercial on the box last night and it was awful/dreadful/pathetic/the pits. I can scarcely bear to tell you but it went like this. . . ."

After this you should be able to go on and fill in what you heard and saw. The chances are you'll choose a commercial that has none of the hallmarks of a well-structured commercial, none of the ingredients that make a commercial work, none of those worthwhile qualities that make it persuasive and a delight to watch.

Go ahead and do it now. Put this book down and try it. If the commercial is as bad as you think it is, then you'll have the devil's own job to put it down into words. You'll probably give up in disgust.

And you know now what you will have proved: a bad commercial is indescribable. Indescribably bad. So bad that you literally can't describe it.

Just to recover your faith in the medium, we'll try the same thing again, but this time we'll try with a commercial you really like. The kind you wish you'd written.

This time you start off your scenario like this: "You missed a really good commercial last night. Great/super/cool/switched on, it was. You should have seen it. It was about this . . ." and then you go on to describe what you saw and heard and how the commercial ended up.

You'll find it so simple compared with the commercial you loved to hate. You'll even remember the name of the product, where you can get it, and how much it costs - if the commercial gives you this information. You may not get it exactly right, especially if it's a brand new product, but you'll get close enough to make the shop assistant understand what you're talking about if it's something you want to buy.

Go on, try it now. Prove it for yourself. Good commercials are simpler to write than bad ones.

It's simple but not easy

No one said it would be easy. But once you know how, it becomes easier. And the way to make it easier is to keep it simple.

Good commercials are simple commercials, simply told.

Writing them is like drawing a circle that takes thirty seconds to complete. Or forty, or sixty, according to the time length your *media department* has bought for you.

It starts off from some point, goes somewhere, and ends up relating to where it started.

A great big O.

There's nothing complicated about it. It isn't a play; it hasn't got a difficult plot, and there's no character development - no time for that. Just a situation that unfolds, develops, and comes to a conclusion. A simple, easily-grasped situation or statement with well-stated, believable characters and words, if there are any of either.

And once the time length has run its course, it leaves you with a certain, albeit small, satisfaction; you gained something from watching it. Perhaps the pleasure was in the situation, the characters, the reality, the story, the twist at the end – whatever it was it left you feeling well-disposed towards, and better-informed about, the product.

But you don't need telling that. You know, instinctively. You've watched enough commercials as an outsider, a consumer. Enough to know what kind of commercial it is that you respond to positively.

You haven't had your clear-eyed, clear-viewing mind complicated and confused by the different considerations that press hard on the TV copywriter inside the advertising agency.

You're on the clear, uncomplicated outside – and that gives you an advantage. Keep your mind as uncomplicated as the consumer's and the way to success as a TV copywriter is as clear as a new motorway before they cut the ribbon.

The big O

Let's get back to the big O.

You may not know at first how or where your commercial is going to start. But one thing you do know is where and how it's going to finish: it's going to finish with the product or something about the product, some way or other.

That's the end of the commercial. You know where you're going and you know the story you have to tell on the way. And you know that wherever you start and whatever you start with you have to relate to the conclusion.

In between the beginning and the end there are 30 seconds (or whatever timelength) of storyline. A simple story it's going to be, simply told in words and/or pictures. So simple you'll find it easy to describe into your tape-recorder.

It will, of course, take longer than 30 seconds to describe – maybe four or five minutes – but that's OK so long as you run the commercial through in your mind's eye – in the TV set that you have built into your head. And you time it with the stop-watch facility on your £2.99 digital watch.

Pretty soon, if you practise your mind's eye televiewing often enough, you'll learn to "feel" what thirty seconds of commercial time feels like.

And just as important, you'll begin to feel the shape that a good commercial has. It's a definite shape. A pattern of events, if you like, that's as old as the art of telling a joke.

It is, in fact, the pattern and shape you would recognise in all the good, easy-to-tell jokes. It's the old "one, two, three – punchline!" pattern.

It's the bedtime story for children. It's the demagogue's urge to action. It's "Liberté, Fraternité, Egalité!"

Striking a chord

You shape your commercial, then, as if you were telling a joke. Or telling a fairy story. But most of all like playing a chord of music.

Let me explain, just in case you never grew up with a piano in the house and don't have your own electronic keyboard.

There's something in music called a major chord. In the key of C it looks like this on a sheet of music.

(Major chord)

If you don't have any kind of musical instrument or can't read music, find someone who has and can. Ask him to play for you this chord of C as an arpeggio, as separate notes starting with the bottom note.

The chord consists of the notes C, E, G, and C an octave higher.

Learn to play it yourself. Play it again and again. Remember it.

44

Get the feel of it. C – E – G – C. One, two, three, one.

And you'll hear and begin to sense the shape that a good commercial will have. Learn this shape and you're more than halfway to making your ideas work.

Think of your commercial expressed musically.

C: the first note is where your commercial starts.

E: the second note grows from and adds interest to what you've already heard.

G: the third note takes what you've heard so far, adds to it, develops it, makes it more interesting, and leads you on to feel a need for –

C: the first note again, resolving the tension created by the first three sounds. Just like the end of the commercial: the end relates to the beginning but in arriving at it you've experienced a totally complete and rewarding experience of the commercial kind.

It is so important that I'll say it again: get this shape into your head and you are months if not years ahead of the average beginner in solving the biggest problem that even experienced creatives have when writing a commercial: the problem of writing to time length. They find it a problem because they don't have the secret of this shape, this feel, this sound structure in their heads. They probably don't even know it exists. But you do.

The music of persuasion

The power of this magic shape is something that few creative men understand, appreciate, or master. They don't understand its magic, its persuasive, seductive power.

It is a basic story-telling force which you must practise to control. When you do you'll be a commercial-writing magician.

Test it for yourself. What are the commercials you like? Which commercials leave you feeling they've been worth watching even if you aren't in the market for the product? Which leave you cold? Which leave you unmoved, disappointed, dissatisfied, even when the commercial is about a product you are interested in buying?

The commercials you like, the commercials that have done something for you, are the commercials that will have the magic shape – even if they have nothing else.

The shape is the music of seduction, unseen perhaps by the viewer, but felt like an emotion, moving, seducing, persuading, affecting the senses. Just like the great and basic musical idea that it is.

Perhaps this will explain to you why the jingle is the most effective vehicle TV advertising has ever adopted. So many times the jingle saves the commercial, not because it is a great jingle, but because at least it has the shape that satisfies, even if the commercial itself hasn't. Now you know why jingle writers make so much money.

Perhaps it also explains why so many of the top TV copywriters are music lovers, musicologists, or part-time musicians.

Variations on a theme

Like all musical ideas, the magic shape for the 30-second commercial is capable of extension, diminution, or adaptation to other lengths.

There is, for example, a musical shape for the 20-second commercial. It looks like this:

(Stave with middle C)

C: this is the opening thought or statement.

46

(Stave with G)

G: an important, "dominant" idea to extend the opening thought which leads you immediately and dramatically to –

(Stave with C octave)

The restatement of the opening idea but with the development of the C and G adding meaning.

Similarly there is a musical shape for the 40-second commercial. It looks like this:

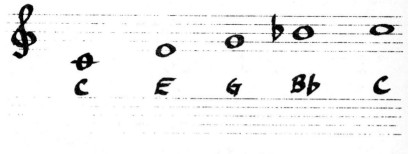

(Arpeggio of C7)

C: this is the opening thought or statement.

E: this is a new thought to develop the first thought.

G: an important, dominant idea extending the developing shape.

B: the beginning of the resolution, adding suspense before –

C: the final resolution of the original idea.

Play that on your keyboard or Schott's C ♯♯ recorder and you'll understand what so few TV commercial writers understand: a 40-second commercial doesn't just have more words than a 30-second commercial; it uses the extra time to dramatise the idea more effectively, not to put in more ideas!

After that a 60-second commercial is simple, a matter of stating and restating for dramatic effect the opening statements – never adding more statements, just restating your two opening thoughts, C and E, then resolving them directly through G to C or via B to C.

It all sounds a bit mathematical and formularised, doesn't it? But then, so is music when you get down to it. But listen to good music – jazz or pop or classical – and you'd never think so. It's just good and satisfying to listen to.

Get these shapes, these magic shapes, into your brain and your friends may still laugh when you sit down at the piano, but their laughter will turn to amazement when you sit down and write a great TV commercial.

Be honest with yourself

One last thing in this chapter: be honest when you run the commercial through in your mind. Never, never, never deceive yourself about how long it takes.

Be certain that your commercial takes 30 seconds and no longer. Use the voice-over you've written, if you have written one, to test the length. Read it out loud, imitate sound effects, make movements with your hands and body to imitate, time, and control the speed of action. Do all this at an honest speed – which means slower than you think it should be. Then you won't fool yourself about the time your actions, even the smallest actions, take.

Be honest with yourself, because the average TV copywriter is never honest with himself. Wishful thinking more than accurate timing is what keeps him going right into the kind of mess that they struggle to put right on the *studio floor* and in the *editor's cutting room*.

To be accurate and honest is more than the average writer's bigger-than-average ego can tolerate. If anything goes wrong, then a huge self-protective mechanism slams into action and everything that goes wrong thenceforth is blamed on the philistines around him or her.

By philistines, the writer usually means the *non-creative people*, including the client, who is always in the wrong – except when he approves the worst commercial that has ever been conceived. Then the idiot client suddenly finds he is a man of super-intelligence and extraordinary perception and sensitivity.

Poor client. Few creative people ever give him credit for being averagely intelligent, for knowing the product or the market, for knowing what he or she wants the product to be. Alas, giving the client what is asked for is anathema to the average copywriter. Which seems to mean that what the client wants is always wrong.

Summary

* *Remember the big O. Make the end relevant to the beginning.*

* *Give your commercial dramatic structure with the magic shape.*

* *The magic shape helps control your idea and your commercial.*

* *The magic shape also makes it easier to write to length.*

* *But always time your commercial honestly. Read it aloud, mime the action. Read, mime, and time.*

Date: 9th January 1987
Client: PILKINGTON GLASS
Product: Corporate

Title:
Length: 60 seconds

Picture

Open on a presenter in limbo. He is
addressing camera. During the
commercial we cut back and forth
between the presenter and a man in a
suit some distance away who is
assembling a rifle. First the stock,
then the silencer and the sights.
He loads the gun.

Sound

Presenter: There aren't
many things today in which
Britain leads the world. Our
motorcyle industry has almost
vanished, our shipbuilding industry
is not what it used to be, but
there is one area in which Britain
not only leads the world but is
actually growing stronger every
day.

You may not have noticed it because
the product is often invisible.
Glass.

In recent years Pilkington,
Britain's leading glass company has
risen from being number four in the
world to number one.

Today Pilkington is the biggest
most successful flat glass compnay
in the world.

The presenter points his finger into
the camera.

With products like ...fibre
optics...opthalmics...camera
lenses...and even more...

We see the presenter through the
sight of the gun, the man in the
suit shoots towards the presenter
and the bullet is stopped by a glass
screen we had not noticed before.
It was not an attempt on the
presenter's life, but a planned
demonstration all along!

The presenter turns and looks at the
mark on the glass next to him.
He nods towards the man who fired
the gun as if to say "thank you".

...bullet resistant glass.

Cut to the Pilkington logo and the
words: The world's leading glass
company.

Pilkington. The world's
leading glass company.

50

An outstanding demonstration for Pilkington Glass, this commercial also demonstrates perfectly the importance of shape, of dramatic structure, and that the best ideas are the simplest to express in storyboard (if you must) or words. Agency: Saatchi & Saatchi Compton. Creatives: Simon Dicketts, Fergus Fleming.

5

How to Win
an Award

You've learned about the magic shape. You've learned the power of its cadence, its in-built rhythm. You've learned how to control the length of your idea by using the shape and measuring it against the spoken words, the mimed actions, and the sound effects that you've written into the commercial.

You've learned that you mustn't fool yourself. That you must be honest. You've realised that you must be murderously honest in your own judgement of the value of your own ideas, measuring them against your experience as a TV-watching consumer, against those values you acquired before you became a TV copywriter.

You're going to hold on tenaciously to that powerful critical ability that's been born and bred into you over the years of critical, consumerist viewing.

You've got all that, so now let's look further than the mechanics of writing a TV commercial and ask: what is it that makes some commercials the commercials that everyone talks about? The commercials that people enjoy seeing, the commercials that make advertising award-giving juries go weak at the knees as they experience uncontrollable, even envious, frissons of admiration. The commercials that make the copywriter famous.

These commercials – *award-winning commercials* – usually have the second of three ingredients that go towards making a TV commercial effective. This is not to say that an award-winning commercial is not an effective commercial. Nor does it mean that an effective commercial cannot win an award. Effective commercials often do, but not as often as award-winning commercials, if you see what I mean.

However, that second important ingredient is this: single-mindedness. What a one-time copy chief of mine called integrity.

She meant a oneness, a wholeness, not only in content but in execution. A totally centred approach which produces a concentrated impact upon the viewer. Everything in the commercial connects. And that's one of the main aims of writing a TV commercial. To connect, to make contact with the customer.

These commercials never waver from the central issue of their idea. The famous Hovis commercials had it; so too did Heineken, Cockburn, John Smith's Bitter.

Such uncompromising clarity of intent and expression is rare. So rare that the majority of awards won in any year are won by a small minority of creatives. The same names crop up again and again. The same people walk into the spotlight each year.

A sense of creative integrity is obviously very rare in the advertising agency business. And so it's no wonder that the judges and the juries who labour at award-giving events are so relieved, moved even, by such rare uncompromising statements that their judgement as businessmen (and some of them are chairmen of their own companies), their commercial judgement, sinks without trace in the swollen sea of their emotional response.

Integrity, in the be-true-to-the-idea sense, is what marks out award-winning quality.

So if you want to aspire only to writing award-winning TV commercials, consider integrity in its many senses as an essential second ingredient which you must add to the first, basic ingredient – the magic shape.

Consider these two ingredients. If you strive for them both – shape and integrity – then you will find it very difficult indeed to write something that does not have that one certain hallmark of the great commercial: genuineness. The real reality in advertising. The touch of understanding and apparent familiarity with the realities of life as she is lived or fantasised.

I'll buy that

Perhaps one of the strangest manifestations of the award-winning commercial is the reaction of the consumer to it.

There it is, a perfect piece of film-craft, beautifully written and structured, altogether beautifully produced with the consummate skill and care that marks out the British Film Industry. And what does it sell? It sells itself.

Too often award-winning commercials are the commercials that make the viewer say: "I'll buy that". The commercial, that is, not the product. It's the commercial they enjoy. It's the commercial that is so complete in itself, so perfectly produced and satisfying to watch that it produces satisfaction of a vicarious kind. "I would like a Martini" becomes "I enjoyed that Martini commercial." The commercial satisfies; you don't need the product. The commercial break is, indeed, the pause that refreshes. Rewards. Satisfies. Produces a kind of hush in your sitting room while it is on. Commercials like the delightful award-winning Hovis commercials – full of sepiated nostalgia but close enough to social history to be credible; the upper-crust Cockburn commercials, played out like some time-warped Ealing Studios comedy. You have only to look in the current *British Design and Art Direction* annual (see Bibliography) and you'll find a whole library of commercials that win awards for their shape and integrity and which tend, thus, to become products in their own right.

I've often thought there might be a market for a video of "Your favourite top 60 TV ads."

But don't misunderstand what is being said here. I have the greatest admiration for those who write TV commercials with care and attention to filmic detail and effect; and especially for those people who produce them with perhaps even greater skill, care, and attention to detail and effect. (You haven't seen anything until you've seen the rigorous titivating of a props person as he or she prepares a pack or some other prop for the camera; or a sound man or woman holding up a very expensive shoot with total conviction that he or she can hear some sound outside the sound-proofed studio, a sound harder for normal human beings to hear than a dog whistle.)

The point to be made here is that some commercials take themselves out of their creator's hands. They become entities in their own right. They exist as something apart from their commercial function. And there is very little one can do about it. You just have to put up with having written a commercial that has become an all-time favourite commercial and hope that it has something in it that rubs off on to the product. How to do that comes in the next chapter.

Go after awards; after all everyone does. But remember this. Award-winning commercials are a celebration of perfected technique, not an indicator of effectiveness in the market place. Another ingredient has still to be added in order to achieve that.

Summary:

* *Write to the magic shape.*

* *Remember what it was like before you became a TV copywriter.*

* *Make your commercial single-minded.*

* *Make it relate to the "realities" of life, real realities or fantasy.*

* *Awards aren't everything – but they have a very pleasant affect upon your salary.*

6

Great Commercial!

"Wish I'd thought of that!"

Awards are a celebration of technique, not an indicator of success in the market place. Don't ever forget that. And don't ever lose your head if you find that you have written a TV commercial that wins an award, or you'll lose the head start that I've given you.

I'd like to think that the commercials you are going to write will be great commercials that happen to win awards because they have lots of that second ingredient – integrity.

There are people, believe it or not, who set out to write award-winning commercials. They've not only lost their heads, they've lost their way, seduced by the prospect of a trip to Cannes at the agency's expense, the spotlit walk down the aisle to collect the award, and one foot on the stairway to that rarified state of life when they can bully clients into accepting every idea they present, with their reputation and their framed awards preceding them. To those people these trips rarely happen.

They more often happen to those who set out to write great commercials and nearly succeeded in doing so; the award that comes their way is – and most of them know it – a consolation prize.

In other words, there's nothing wrong with award-winning commercials except that they aren't necessarily great commercials.

"Great!" is a word you hear very often in an advertising agency, which is where you will be writing your TV commercials.

It's an old-timer of a word, but everybody seems to use it at times of high, Krakatoan emotion; that is, when they've just been privileged to witness the birth or the realisation of a good idea.

"Great commercial!" is the highest accolade. Unsurpassable.

Unless it is repeated twice: "Great commercial!"; a slight pause and then again: "Great commercial!"

The first time this is said to you, you probably won't know how to cope. Perhaps you didn't think it was great. Just good, you know, all right, well, good. But then it suddenly becomes great when it's exposed to the world for the first time. Marvellous moment. But how do you make it happen for you?

The third ingredient

What is it that makes a commercial great?

A great commercial has three ingredients:

1. It has the magic shape; it is structurally correct.

2. It has integrity; a unique oneness of product, idea, and execution.

3. It expresses a simple benefit clearly and competitively.

In three paragraphs I have exposed the mystery of the craft of writing TV commercials. But were you listening?

Read them again, and then read them again. And underline them in red or cover them with yellow from one of those felt tips used by eager young account executives to emphasise the most brilliant passages in the memos they write.

What was it those three paragraphs said? What did I say makes a great commercial? I don't mean a commercial. I don't mean an award-winning commercial. I mean a great commercial!

I'll ask the printer to print the figures again, complete with dotted lines after each figure so that you can write down in your own words the answer to the question I ask you again. What three ingredients make a great commercial?

1 ....

....

2 ....

....

3 ....

....

Finished? Sure? Now compare your answers with my three paragraphs.

If you didn't get them down word for word, tippex your answers out and do it again! And again, until you get it right. Dead right.

Now, if you've got the words right, I'll make sure you understand what they mean. Let's take them one by one.

1. The magic shape is that mysterious feel or sound, something very much akin to a major arpeggio in music, which leads the viewer on by irresistible steps to a satisfactory and satisfying conclusion, taking the viewer to an end that he or she feels is inevitable and inexplicably right, complete, and inescapable. Without it you haven't got a commercial worth running.

2. Integrity is that quality of oneness, unity. To get it, you will have to lean on everything and everyone – including, and most of all, yourself – with dedication and conviction until you get a commercial in which every single second of picture and sound concentrates on achieving one all-important impact on the viewer's mind. Integrity means oneness, single-mindedness, everything connecting. Without it, you'll never win an award.

3. A simple benefit expressed simply and clearly is the most difficult ingredient to find. It is what makes a great commercial. And it's the trick that's the hardest to turn.

Stay a consumer

How do you go about finding that all-important third ingredient?

First, you've got to know your product. And you've got to believe that it has a reason for existing. Every product on the shelves, or in the showroom, has a reason for being there. It's the product of someone having the idea producing a product that some people will want more than any other product of its kind; something they'd rather spend their money on than anything else.

I repeat: every product has a reason for existing. If it dies, becomes commercially unviable, it's because not enough people thought the product offered anything worth having. Not enough people wanted, or could afford, to buy it. That is why a small domestic market like Britain has a product failure rate of something approaching 80%. In a huge home market like the United States, the figure is lower simply because there's a four times bigger chance of finding a market that will support any given product.

Your job is to isolate what it is about that product that creates its audience, and to present its unique quality in such a way that your target audience is absolutely clear as to how it will benefit them.

That's all.

To help you, I remind you of the head-start you've got over the people who have been doing this kind of thing for years.

You are fresh from the viewing side of the screen. You are still a consumer. Just hang on to that. Stay a consumer. And don't pull a fast one on yourself when you set out to find a simple benefit that you, at the consumer level, would like to be told about.

Make it an honest benefit; that goes without saying. One you would accept if you were part of the target audience. Make it connect with real-life experience or expectations, not the life experience and expectation that bad commercials present to you.

It can be based in seriousness, or in fun, real or surreal. But it mustn't be phoney.

Say it simply and honestly.

"Prolongs active life" is the famous dog food USP (see below). *"Helps you work, rest, and play"* *"Re-record ... not fade away, re-record ... not fade up."*

Make it a specific benefit that belongs to, or is made – by force of money or by supreme creativity – to belong to a particular product.

Make it a benefit that is a better benefit, or a different benefit from the benefit offered by any products competing in the same *product category*. Make it different enough and you create your own category – and life becomes so much easier for everyone.

The benefit can be different, unexpected, novel, outrageous. But never less than honest, "true" to whatever aspect of life the product belongs in. If it's dishonest or unrealistic, the product will die a faster than natural death; advertising works, you know, but not always in the way you would like it to. Money doesn't always buy belief and conviction; it can buy sudden death.

Try to make your benefit one that doesn't need explaining. Doesn't need a reason why. That's the best kind of benefit – an obvious, self-evident, competitive benefit. One that doesn't need an explanation or justification.

You'll often hear talk of finding a *USP*. The initials stand for *Unique Selling Proposition*, perhaps the greatest advertising idea of all time, created by Rosser Reeves to promote the particular approach of the Ted Bates advertising agency in America. Misunderstood by almost everyone outside Ted Bates from the day of its inception, it is used carelessly by everyone in the advertising business to mean an advertising idea, and used so frequently – even in the promotional literature of other agencies – that Rosser Reeves would have made a few more millions than he did if he had been able to copyright his idea.

Unique means a particular something about the product that is or can be made to appear unique to the product.

Selling means that this particular something must have a selling power inherent in it that constitutes a benefit.

Proposition means a presentation of this unique and beneficial characteristic in a form of words that is distinctive and memorable and clearly states the benefit.

The USP is perhaps the only worthwhile formula ever created for undoubtedly successful advertising. There have been many attempts to imitate and improve on it, but none of them have lasted the course.

Like most formulae, it produced formularised work, rigidly examined – often by criteria the originator would have rejected – with the result that so-called USP advertising became petrified in the period in which it was created – the hungry, intensely "we can't take risks or make mistakes" 1950s.

Big businesses were built on its solid foundations and still exist as powerful forces in the market. Consequently there are still examples of USP advertising on our screens today, albeit tentatively and superficially up-dated in an attempt to fit the culture of the 1980s.

The sad and significant thing is that this great idea, this amazing, fundamental understanding of the selling – buying process, was not allowed to develop its own truth. The practitioners of USP advertising did not realise, as you realise, that advertising is part of our lives. It is there every night. It is an ingredient in the nightly and now daily culture of 90% of the nation. It has its own force and contribution to make in moulding our way of life.

When you write your commercials you will realise this – after all it's not so long ago that you were experiencing this phenomenon as a consumer; consequently, you know better than most.

You will realise that your commercial has to be in touch with real life. It has to connect. It can't be a rigid, sterile, stereotyped process. It has to have a living, human, contemporary content.

But this does not mean that you must consign the idea of the USP to history. It is a fundamental idea. What I suggest is you buy Rosser Reeves's book, *Reality in Advertising*, study it, understand it, and apply its basic ideas in a contemporary way.

If you like, think of the Unique Selling Proposition as Unique Buying Proposition; this will help to throw the emphasis on the consumer's needs, and remove it from the seller's imperative.

It will also help you to arrive at that Third Ingredient, the simple, self-evident benefit that distinguishes your product from any other. And, in doing so, it will help you create advertising that is distinctive and competitive.

So there you have it. Read every word of this book again and you'll find that nowhere did I say it would be easy. Simple, yes. Easy? No.

But look at it like this. At least you now have the benefit of knowing what it is you are to look for when you come to write that great TV commercial. Most writers haven't a clue.

So, hard as it may seem at first, it's that much easier for you because, like a good commercial, you know where you are going.

After only six chapters you are already streets ahead of those in the game.

That's the benefit of this book!

Summary

* *Every product has a reason for existing. Find out what it is.*

* *Find a simple benefit, preferably one that doesn't need justifying or explaining.*

* *Present it clearly, simply, honestly.*

* *Put it into a magic shape.*

* *Tell it with integrity, oneness, unity.*

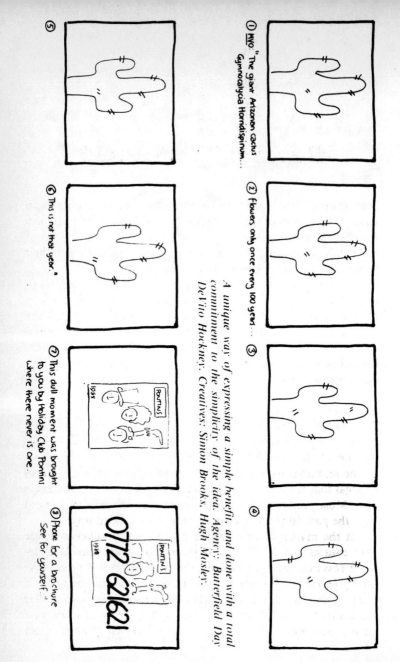

① MVO: "The giant Arizonan cactus Gymnocalycia Horridispinum....

② flowers only once every 100 years....

⑥ This is not that year."

⑦ This dull moment was brought to you by Holiday Club Pontins where there never is one.

⑧ Phone for a brochure. See for yourself."

A unique way of expressing a simple benefit, and done with a total commitment to the simplicity of the idea. Agency: Butterfield Day DeVito Hockney. Creatives: Simon Brooks, Hugh Mosley.

7

Research: Who Needs It?

It is inevitable that a company spending huge sums of money on an advertising campaign should want to feel fairly sure that the money is going to be well spent.

That is to say, most clients are prepared to settle for their advertising budget not being totally wasted.

"I know," said Lord Leverhulme, founder of the great soap-making company, "that half my advertising spend is wasted. I wish I knew which half." That was said before the days of research, in the days when men of industry had vision and enterprise – and a fairly easy market, virtually a commercial vacuum, into which they could drop their new-technology products knowing that a rising middle-class and an aspirational blue-collar class would buy.

The competition between products was minimal. The competition between advertisements was equally so.

All the research needed then was research based upon one man's instinct for what would sell.

Now, of course, it's different.

The market-place is jammed. A technological breakthrough so original that it creates a new product category or a new market is rare. Most products are like the car engine – basically unchanged over the past 50 years, improved only in peripheral ways.

Yet the market-place continues to expand. Products that are close cousins survive side by side, promoted and kept alive by a life-support system called advertising, the most powerful of which is the kind you want to learn how to write: television advertising.

Every product, as was said earlier, has a reason for existing. The successful television commercial is the one that identifies that reason and makes it meaningful to a sufficiently large target audience for the product to flourish.

But, and here's the big question, how do you know when you've found that reason for existing, that reason for buying?

The writer of the television commercial, someone like you, someone in touch with the common consumer, has the answer ready and pat. Relying upon his instincts, like the entrepreneur of old, the writer will say: "I just know. I know people. I know that what I've written about the product will be meaningful to customers out there." A bit like Shakespeare and his plays.

But, unlike the entrepreneur of old, the writer doesn't have the millions needed to back his instincts in the market place. It is the client who has those millions at his disposal. The client, however, is responsible to his board and his shareholders for being right – or wrong. He is not, like the entrepreneurs of old, the master of his own business destiny.

So what would you do if you were the client?

You'd say to the writer: prove it. Prove that what you want me to spend millions on will actually move potential consumers into becoming actual consumers. That's all the client wants: proof, preferably in writing. A piece of paper to legitimise the decision he makes.

In other words, he wants research to show that the commercial is going to work. And can you blame him? After all, it's not his money. But it is his job.

What is research?

First of all, let's consider what research is not.

Research is not a substitute for courage. It is not a substitute for faith in personal judgement. It is not always a cop-out and a last hiding place for the client who can't protect himself from the insistence of the agency. And it need not be a pair of expensive manacles chaining the wrists of the TV commercial writer.

What it can be is an exploration of the limits of creativity in any given area. It can be a way of redefining methods and techniques, and of investigating the rate of development of social and cultural responses.

It can be all these things if – and it is a big if – research is used to find out what is right about a TV commercial and not only what is wrong about it.

This, of course, requires a new kind of courage, ability, and vision. It requires judgement in the interpretation of the research findings, a sensitive process of decision-making which commits the client to proceeding or not.

By using research, the decision to approve the commercial or not is, admittedly, simply postponed until after another stage has been reached; the waiting can be justified.

Having said what research is not, and what it can be, let's look at what it actually is and does.

What research measures

Research is a means of measuring the effectiveness of a commercial against what the commercial is written to achieve.

The criteria for judging the commercial are established (usually) before the commercial is written; if you are wise and insistent, you should be among those people who establish those criteria.

What the commercial is intended to achieve is entombed in one or all of three documents, whose names at least you ought to familiarise yourself with:

There's the *marketing strategy*, which is a general statement, backed up with facts and figures, of how the product is to be sold: the kind of product it is to be, the method of distribution, the price, the contents, the potential market, and the competition are all features of this document.

The *advertising strategy* – not as popular a document these days – deals in the basic approach to the advertising and the basic appeals of the product, with perhaps a simple, non-advertising statement of the benefits of the product compared with competitive products.

The third document is variously called the *copy strategy*, the creative brief, or the creative plan, nomenclatures that change from agency to agency. But they all have in common this information:

(a)   the target audience

(b)   a list of benefits and/or *product attributes*

(c)   a simple statement of the main claim, the main area of consumer benefit

(d)   an assessment of what the target audience's response is desired to be after seeing the commercial.*

The purpose of research is to test the degree of effectiveness to which this information has been used.

(a)   Was it accurately aimed at the target audience?

(b)   Did it present the benefits effectively?

(c)   Did it communicate the main claim effectively?

(d)   Did it produce the desired response from the target audience?

Whether or not the commercial satisfied these criteria determines whether or not the commercial is considered to be effective.

Who conducts the research?

Research companies conduct research.

The researcher comes into the agency and is taken through your commercial. The criteria for researching it are made known to the researcher, who then goes away – only to come back a few days later with a proposed method of research, the method which will most rigorously seek out your commercial's deficiencies, proclaim its mediocrity, or celebrate its brilliance.

On the basis of the result, you will find it easy to assess the competence or otherwise of the research company involved!

*There are other statements but none that need bother us at this moment.

Although there is a never-ending variety of new theories and philosophies of research, most research proposals feature one or other of the two methods most commonly used. These are:

(a) Group discussions

(b) Hall tests

Group discussions These are fascinating. They present you with the opportunity of meeting your target audience face to face in small groups of 6-10, never many more. And it's usually in the evening – you have to make some sacrifices for your education – at one of the houses of a member of the group.

The group members – your target audience, remember, carefully selected by your research company – are paid a small fee. And they are usually determined to earn it by becoming experts on TV commercials for the evening: what they think of commercials; which ones are good, which ones bad; and how they could do better.

And they are always right. To you, the writer, they may be wrong. But they are always right. Because they are the customer – and you know what they say about the customer.

If it's your commercial you are privileged to hear them tearing to pieces, then you just have to sit and bear it.

Hang on to that grin, no matter how much it starts to hurt, and don't resort to physical violence, or your research man will never ask you to one of his group discussions again.

Don't argue, just listen. The research man will do the probing, the questioning, the querying, the coaxing. You just sit there and learn what you already know, and take comfort in the fact that this isn't the only group of target customers to be given a chance to appraise your commercial. There will be other groups, all over the country, to make the research representative. In Enfield your research man may have discovered an epidemic of morons, but up in Wilmslow, there could be a half a dozen people who are as bright as blazer buttons and love the idea of your commercial to death. This north–south split is a common phenomenon and it has frequently condemned or saved a writer's commercial, according to the research man's interpretation of where the mean lies.

Hall tests These are less fascinating, but a better night out.

Hall tests take place, as you would imagine, in halls up and down the country – usually, in my experience, town halls, where the seating is comfortable and the projection facilities are better than average.

What happens is this. By a process of screening and selection, an audience is invited to what is thinly disguised as an evening's "entertainment" at whatever venue has been chosen. There they are served coffee and tea and biscuits and then asked to fill in certain research questionnaires which will reveal their attitudes towards a variety of subjects, including products in certain categories.

Then follow a number of short films interlaced with commercials, the commercial you have written among them. A different questionnaire is then distributed, the purpose of which is to discover whether their attitude and understanding of the products involved have changed, and what effect the commercial you wrote has had upon them: whether they remember seeing it at all, what they remember best about it, and so on.

This ritual is, as with group discussion, carried out at a number of centres and the results are collated, examined, and discussed back at the agency and with the client.

As you've probably guessed already, the hall test and the group discussion serve two different purposes.

The group discussion is used mainly to test ideas in script and storyboard form, while the hall test is used to examine the completed, filmed commercial so that further refinements can be made to it before it is broadcast.

That's all you need to know about research. There is a great deal more made of it, but then that's someone else's concern. Your concern is preparing the idea you have for successful research.

Preparing for research

The preparation of material for the hall tests is out of your hands. The film is made, perhaps only in a *rough cut* version, but it is complete as far as research is concerned.

Preparation for the group discussions, however, is a different matter and you should be very much involved. You should be involved because what you want is that your commercial idea gets the best possible reception.

How do you do this?

Early in this book the shape of the commercial was discussed – the value of a simple self-evident benefit, the value of simplicity and integrity in the idea.

This is what you have to concentrate on expressing in your script/storyboard preparation for research. You will be sorely tempted to try to include all the *production values* you want so desperately to express – but don't. Don't even try to. Stick with expressing the simple idea and try to do it in no more than four single frames; that is to say, four illustrations each depicting the main action events in the commercial.

If your idea has the magic shape, has observed the value of a simple self-evident benefit and the value of simplicity and integrity in the idea, you'll be able to restrict your idea to four frames easily.

The whole idea, you see, is to make it simple. Simple for the researcher to present to the group of interviewees, and simple for them to grasp.

Anything complicated, and the researcher will fall over his tongue trying to explain all the complexities and nuances that only film can express; or else he'll convey the beautifully wrought atmosphere that you hope will be evident in your finished commercial as if he were describing an old boot that's been left out in the rain.

Save your Fellini moments for the actual production; your *film director* is so much better at it than any researcher. That's why they can afford to own racehorses, Elizabethan manor houses, and the manor that goes with them.

The scenario

One of the good things Saatchi & Saatchi did for the advertising business, I believe, was to introduce the idea of the scenario as a means of researching commercials at the idea stage.

It is cheap to prepare, it allows a far better presentation of the whole idea – and it gives the writer of the commercial almost total control over its presentation to the consumer.

Why clients are, generally, distrustful of it, I cannot fathom. It saves them money and it is proven to be as effective – I believe more effective – than anything short of the completed film.

From the presentation point of view, it is certain and consistent because it can be taped – indeed, it is essential that it is taped, and played back on a simple cassette player. There is no variation in the researcher's ability to present it on any given off or on night, and no variation between researchers themselves when groups are being held at several different locations by different researchers.

From the point of view of presenting the idea, it leaves the storyboard method standing; there's no dependence upon a very unpredictable graphic presentation and no cumbersome boards to carry around and put on display. There is no chance of the commercial's reception being affected by the unpredictable predilection of consumers for tall, dark men or short, blonde women.

Perhaps more important, the scenario doesn't mould the finished film into an image not of its own likeness. An idea for a commercial is a fragile thing. Writers are often mistakenly accused of sloth and slowness, when what is really happening is something quite different: when they have an idea in their mind, a good idea, a really good idea, they are reluctant to commit it to paper, fearful that in the translation from thought to words it will disappear, change, lose its quality. To take it yet another stage further and allow a storyboard artist to interpret it through his mind can lose the idea's integrity almost immediately. To see it set down at this early stage can sometimes destroy it. Far better to leave it in the descriptive words of the author as they come straight from his mind.

This is a hard argument to make to anyone other than a writer, because it is only a writer's experience. If I'm wrong and discover that it is a phenomenon that others in the commercial-making process understand, then I would be delighted. And so should you be.

Summary

*   *Go to group discussions and listen. Don't argue.*

*   *Go to hall tests, and evaluate the procedure for yourself.*

*   *Be there when the criteria for testing are established.*

*   *Write simply for research – embellishments, refinements come later.*

*   *Sneer at storyboards. Promote scenarios – the pictures you paint with words are better.*

8

Making Your Commercial

Once upon a time, in the bad old days, a writer wasn't allowed near the *production* of the commercial he had written. Regardless of the fact that it wouldn't have existed if the writer hadn't written it. Regardless of the fact that the writer was the one who knew exactly what it should look like.

Then came the time – it lasted for a brief period only – when the writer became the *producer* too, and the producer was relegated to being a production assistant, a gofer, the person who literally carried the can of film backwards and forwards between the agency and the cutting room.

That didn't work, mainly because the work of the producer is time-consuming and the cost of the writer is expensive. Why have a writer walking around the streets of Soho when he could be back at his desk writing great commercials?

But I suspect that what really brought that period to an end was the discovery by the active-minded writer that making a television commercial was actually very boring. Unutterably boring. A waste of his valuable time. That's what the producer was paid to endure – and they seem to enjoy it.

No doubt the first couple of times, you might find it fun. But thereafter, I hope not. A writer enjoying the shooting of a commercial indicates either a complete lack of a sense of the proper importance of things, or an incomplete social life. Because that's how your time on the studio floor is taken up – in socialising.

You have a greater role to play, a role no one else has: writing more great commercials.

But do not misunderstand me. I do not suggest that you have nothing to do with the production of your commercial at all.

Indeed, no. Your role is vital, but it is well-defined.

The role of the writer

You have written your commercial. It has survived research, even benefited from creative interpretation of that research, and has been approved by the client. It is still recognisable as the commercial you laboured over and still love.

Spread before you is all that world-stunning talent of the British Film Industry – and between it and you there is only your agency producer.

Which production company to choose? Which *director's reel* to see? Who to cast? Which *voice-over* is equal to your script?

These are the decisions to be made – and you must make sure that you are on hand to help make them. You may be only a beginner at the game, but you have one inescapable, irrefutable qualification that weighs as heavily as any producer's experience and knowledge: you wrote it, he didn't.

Luckily, there are few production autocrats left. The mystique of film making, the buzz words, the abbreviations, the argot, have all been penetrated. Even *graduate trainees* know them as if they had breathed them in with the Oxbridge air.

So there's nothing you need to know that you won't learn within two months or two short visits to someone else's production. There's lots more to know, but that's for directors and producers to know. You don't need it.

What you need to bring to the process of production is your knowledge of the commercials you've seen on the box. Chances are that you've written the kind of commercial you like to watch. What you may not know is that one of the reasons why you like to watch it is because of the way the director has *shot* it.

So why not get your producer to find out who shot the commercial you liked and ask to see his reel? Have a look at it with your producer. Ask your producer, if he needs asking, to get in other reels he thinks may be interesting, and by this process decide to speak to one or more of the directors whose work interests you.

The producer will look after the logistics and administration of this.

The production company

To make your commercial you will use a production company. In the current issue of *Creative Handbook* there are 15 pages, with 50 or so to a page, of video and film production companies.

Of these an agency will use about 20 in a year; of these 20, about 5 will be constantly swinging through the door.

So the daunting task of choosing from over 750 possible companies is considerably eased by the working experience of the producer and also by the style of the work the agency does which makes them famous.

The TV commercial directors are usually the founder owners of production companies, or they are "attached" to a particular company. So your choice of director will necessarily result in your meeting the production company in the form of the production company producer – the opposite number to the agency producer, but usually a much jollier sort – and his team.

This is the run up to that part of the process known as *pre-production*. But only the run-up; you have a long way to go yet.

The role of the production company is to assemble the whole *production unit – camera-crew, art director, lighting, props, casting director, actors,* arrange for the *studio, transport, catering –* in fact all those innumerable functionaries and prerequisites to a full-scale film production necessary to turning your idea into a 30″ work of folk art. The production company producer manages all this; and whatever he earns for doing it, he earns every penny: to me it always seemed complex and fraught with potential and actual disaster. Make no mistake, production company producers, in my experience, are the good guys and it's worth getting to know them well.

Choosing a production company

You will realize from the above that, in my view, the production company producer is a key figure in your choice of production company. He is the man who will produce the *quote* for producing the commercial; he will act as a go-between for you and the director; he will sort out problems as and when they arrive. His willingness to do this, his efficiency at doing this, are paramount. A good production company producer clears the way, all the way, for the best possible realization of your script.

Needless to say, there are other considerations. The size of the company sometimes counts. Its size can determine the choice of directors "attached" to them and therefore your choice of director. Its connections abroad can make things easier if you are shooting abroad. Its in-house facilities – its own studio, its own *editing suites,* on-staff *editors*, sometimes even its own *projection room* – can all influence the price and the smoothness of the production.

But big doesn't always mean best for your particular script. The decision not to use a fully-staffed production company gives you the opportunity to choose the various specialists because of their work, not because of the company they work for.

Smaller companies can give you a (real or imagined) sense of greater commitment and involvement. Using independent specialists can add an extra, live ingredient to the mix. All this is difficult to define in theory, but it is something that takes only a short time to appreciate in practice. In the meantime, in your learning stages, trust your producer's opinion and your own feelings – particularly when it comes to making the most important choice of all: which director to choose.

Choosing a director

You've spent hours in the projection room looking at cans and cans of film by a variety of directors.

You've identified a short list of directors whose work interests you – not just because they've directed scripts of the genre you chosen to use, but because they've shown intelligence, film-craft, and creativity in focusing upon and expressing the central idea of the script. And there is in their work that essential for great and award-winning commercials: integrity. Sometimes, despite the complexity of the content of the script, somehow they've managed to make it all of a piece, given it a oneness that makes it all connect.

So you and your producer decide to let, say, three of them look at the script. A meeting is arranged, either at your agency or at their very zizzy suite of offices. Your producer is not the kind of producer who sends scripts unaccompanied and in advance; he knows that you are the kind of writer who likes to *present* the script from your own scenario, the way you presented it to the client.

This way of going about things is essential for two reasons:

1 The director receives the same presentation as the client and the chances are high, therefore, that he will get out of your presentation the same emphases in the same places as the client; ie the director begins to understand what it is the client bought.

2 The director receives direct from you your interpretation of the script so that he understands clearly what you see in the script.

You may feel a bit of a fool having to go through this procedure of presentation perhaps for the fourth or fifth time, but it is crucial that right from the start the director understands how you would direct it if you were clever enough to be a director!

Having established that ground clearly, the director doesn't have to guess at what you have in mind and consequently can then apply himself and his craft to expressing your script in the most relevant and expert way.

The next step is assessing the director's response to the script. All directors, at this stage, will be polite! Ignore that. Listen to the comments they make, the off-the-top ideas for filming it suggests to them, the suggestions for improving the film "language" so that the idea is better articulated; and above all listen for, and beware of, his ideas for changing it into a different script, into the film he would have written if he could.

79

You've done all those things and you've come up with a director you think will shoot your script the way you would like it to be shot. And now you have to decide: is he the kind of director you can talk to?

If he isn't, if the chemistry isn't right – forget it, and start all over again. What you want is a good commercial, not a good fight.

The pre-production meeting

You've chosen your director, you're happy with his production company, the quote has been approved, a shooting date has been pencilled in.

From here onwards, everything happens fairly quickly in a time-established procedure.

A pre-production meeting is held, usually with the client present, but sometimes without. Introductions are made all round. Everyone is friends, everyone is supplied with indifferent coffee, and the director goes through the process of telling the assembled meeting (ie the client) how he intends to shoot the script, shot by shot. (Listen carefully and speak up if there is anything that comes as a surprise!)

Next on the agenda will be any one of the following:

Set design This is self-explanatory. Drawings made by the art director of the various scene locations in which the script is shot are discussed. Your producer will have involved you in their preparation; your view of the first sketches will be the first time you see anything approaching a specific interpretation of your script. It is an important part of the production, so pay careful attention to what is being proposed. Check it against your original conception.

If the art director's ideas expand your idea correctly, fine! But if they change it significantly, say so before the pre-production meeting. Remember, it's still your commercial.

Casting From your brief, a casting session will have been arranged and artists usually videotaped for later viewing. Be there! If you wrote the script with certain types in mind, those are the types you want to see in your film. Stick to your brief. But don't be too adamant. The chances are the director has come across someone new, or someone he's worked with recently, who can enhance the role you've written. Look at his suggestion critically but constructively.

Wardrobe In other words what your actors will be wearing. There'll be a wardrobe person there, hired by the production company. If you know a lot about clothes and clothes design, fine. I don't. So I leave it to the specialists. If only clients would do the same.

Product After all, that's what it's all about: the product. Fascinating, if it's a Ferrari. If it's a can of dog food, slightly less so. The discussion usually involves supplies of a perfect specimen of the pack, but this is where some directors behave beautifully. The attention and interest they give to the subject is such that you'd think they were shooting a Fabergé egg. Their affection and dedication is equalled only by the props person whose job it is to maintain the perfect pack in a state of perfection through every single close-up.

At the end of the pre-production meeting, everyone walks away with a *call sheet.*

If you've found favour your name will be on it, but in such a position that it is made quite clear to you that your role is now totally inferior to everyone else – including the all-important caterers. (There is nothing but nothing so welcome, so delicious, or so essential to life and the production as a hot bacon roll early on the morning of the shoot.)

Sir!

The day of the shoot arrives. For the experience, you are there. The production company producer will be jolly to you and make you feel specially welcome and important to the event, and that you have your bacon roll, but only after the real workers, the unit, have

81

had theirs. You aren't important; the only important man is the director.

This is expressed by a charming convention. On the studio floor, the director is addressed by everyone in the unit as "Sir!"; failing that, "Guvnor", but it is still said in such a way that it might just as well be "Sir!"

This is no forelock-tugging sycophancy or any kind of class struggle going on in what is a highly-unionised context. It is simply a matter of efficiency. Pragmatism.

On the floor the director is like the captain of a ship. You obey him. You do what he says. He is the man. No argument, sir. He is the one man responsible for getting it in the can on the day, within the time. He is the one who is responsible. No one else. Certainly not you.

Another convention, less observed than it should be, is that no one who is not part of the film unit – people like you and the client – should ever speak directly to the director unless invited to do so. Again very sensible and necessary. If you have a comment, make it to your producer, who will then speak to the director, who may then discuss the matter with you.

Once you get on the floor, once you start shooting, it's the director's film for as long as the production lasts. It's not yours, it is not even the client's film – even though he's promised to pay for it.

It is the director's film while he is making it.

In fact, on the floor, you may find him so remote that you may wonder what happened to the cheerful, outgoing cove you met at the pre-production, the one so complimentary about your commercial? He turned back into a professional director, that's what, with a great deal of someone else's money to spend; it's amazing what a responsibility like that can do to one's demeanour.

If he asks your advice or opinion, feel flattered and treat the occasion with the respect it deserves.

The editor

Editors are good guys too. They are stars in their own right with a kind of guildsman's confidence that allows them to be the only ones who can really talk to the director on something approaching his own terms.

This is not surprising, because the editor is a kind of director in his own right, directing the as-shot film footage in his cutting room, in much the same way as the director directs the camera on the floor. Not entirely comparable, but then I am in favour of editors.

The first time you meet the editor will be at the viewing of the *rushes*, very early one morning in Soho or your city's equivalent.

At the rushes, the director, editor, your producer, the production company's producer, and you will see a continuous procession of the *takes* that were selected from the *footage* shot and *printed* hurriedly (in a rush!) for viewing. A further selection is made for *editing* into a rough cut.

This may very well be called the *director's cut*, something you won't be invited to be involved in. Don't be hurt by this craft exclusion. We are dealing in film now, not your script, and it is wise and just that the film-makers should be given a free hand – at first. Look at what they do with your original concept in mind – but don't expect a perfect overlay of what was in your mind's eye. Now is the time to look at it with a fresh eye, and ask yourself: "Is this having the effect upon me that I set out to have upon my viewers? Is this a valid interpretation of what I saw in my mind's eye?" If it is, fine. If it isn't, don't get technical. Just use the words you normally use to explain what it is that doesn't satisfy. After all, it is starting to become your property again and will go on becoming more so as the stages of *post-production* follow, one upon the other.

If you are unhappy with the cut, just remember two things:

1 You can't change the image on the film – well, not without enormous expense.

2 Trust your editor. They may seem just cut-and-stick merchants to you at first, but the experience of working with a talented editor will soon change that idea; what they can do with film is the

ultimate magic.

When the director has contributed all he thinks he can contribute, he'll start thinking about his next commercial/feature film/TV series, leaving you and your producer and your editor to complete the finishing touches. Of all the stages in the production of the commercial, this *fine-cutting* can be the most enjoyable and the most rewarding. This is worth leaving your desk for. This is making film work!

The words...

The right side of the traditional form of script carries all the sound you have written into your commercial: music, voices, sound effects.

Sometimes the *sound track* is recorded before the film is cut, sometimes even before the film is shot, but mostly it is recorded after the film editing process.

Recording involves a *sound studio*, a *sound engineer*, and anything from a single voice to a full symphony orchestra, warm-blooded or synthesised.

My advice is – as always when the interpretation of your script is concerned – be there! The *recording session* may be attended by the director and/or the editor. You will have your producer. In voice recording sessions you will find that the director involves you more directly. Again, hold fast in your mind to your original concept of the script and judge everything against that; but not so rigidly that you close your mind entirely to spontaneous changes of delivery or inflection or pacing. Wonderful things can happen when a good *voice artist* gets hold of a script: delivered slightly differently from the way you conceived them, your words can sound even better than they really are!

...and music

Of all the stages of production of a commercial, recording a music track with real live musicians can be one of the most enjoyable and rewarding. It can also be the one part of the process where you are completely and totally in the hands of the music man!

You will, of course, have had a meeting with him to discuss the main thrust of the commercial and the mood that needs to be conjured up in words, pictures, and music. And, like the professional musical director he is, he will have given you some outline of the musical idea – he will have played it to you on his keyboard. What you make of it in terms of how he will expand it musically is, of course, determined by your musical knowledge. Minimal it might be, but that shouldn't stop you having some opinion on whether you think it is going to sound right. If in doubt, ask, but ask at an early stage, long before you've got your musicians sitting there with the metronome ticking like the meter on a taxi.

Ask early because, when the session starts, you witness the relentless building of a musical maze that to the untechnical can be bewildering.

Once again, trust your music man. If you've briefed him intelligently and fully, there's no other part of the production process you'll enjoy more. Except early morning bacon rolls.

Can you trust your director?

Perhaps I'm wrong. Perhaps the production of a commercial isn't so unutterably boring after all. But my point of view stands. The writer's job is writing TV commercials better than anyone else can. That's his role above all else. Making sure they are produced well is, of course, part of it, but not the first part.

The writer's contribution to the production is to help choose and brief the director, the production company, the cast, the music – and then to trust the people he's chosen to do the job better than he can.

If the writer gets his scenario right, presents it well, then leaves it to the director he has chosen – and trusts him – then he'll get the commercial filmed just the way the writer would film it himself. It may not be exactly the film he would have made if he had been the director; but then the writer is not the director! The director is. And as the writer has chosen the director for what he can do with and for the scenario, then why should the writer try to do it for him? (The client will be the one most likely to try to do this.)

Let the director shoot the film, let the editor cut it, let the music man make the music. Your role is to see that they understand the balance of the commercial in terms of emphasis, mood, meaning; and to make it quite clear that you don't want any of their own little predilections running away with your script.

You'll find this easy with the open-minded sort of director. The kind that doesn't feel so insecure and threatened that he has to play everything close to his chest. The open-minded kind is ready to discuss his *shooting plan* with the writer and his producer. This is important for everyone concerned. The writer will then know what is going to happen, the producer is there to check that it does, and the director is left to do it the way he told you he would.

Typical of this kind of director is the one who puts his cards on the table in such a way that everyone, including the clients, leaves the pre-production meeting smiling and confident. He does this by preparing and presenting to the meeting the only kind of "storyboard" that makes any sense: a director's shooting storyboard. There's an example on page 88.

Look at it. Study it. It will help you to write commercials that make shooting sense. But don't, of course, let it inhibit you. (Nothing should do that where writing a script is concerned. Anything you can imagine clearly in your mind can be transferred to film. Anything.)

End shot

Any honest-minded director or editor will admit that he's primarily concerned with making and cutting a film. You are the one whose first interest should be in making a commercial.

The client, unfortunately, is too often the one who is interested in making something that's a cross between a hectoring piece of propaganda and a sales training film. The really stupid client – there are fewer and fewer of them – demonstrates his lack of confidence in the product, lack of confidence in the medium, and his contempt for the viewer; this client still prefers the wham-bang style of commercial whose effectiveness is evaluated on the basis of the number of "supers" in the 30 seconds and the volume of voices and music.

You're the only one who understands what commercial writing is supposed to be about. You're the one who knows about the power of the magic shape, integrity, and the effectiveness of a simple benefit clearly and competitively expressed.

Don't expect all directors or clients to understand. Remember, you're ahead of them and it's your job to lead them gently, persuasively, effectively along the path of rightness, using tact, understanding, firmness, and your own integrity.

Summary

* *Remember, you know more about the script than anyone.*

* *Be there, always, when the director is chosen.*

* *Present your script to the director, just the way you did to your client.*

* *Listen to what the director has to say; it may be important.*

* *Always be there at the pre-production.*

* *Trust your editor; after all you helped choose him when you chose the director and the production company.*

* *Never, never lose sight of what kind of commercial you meant it to be.*

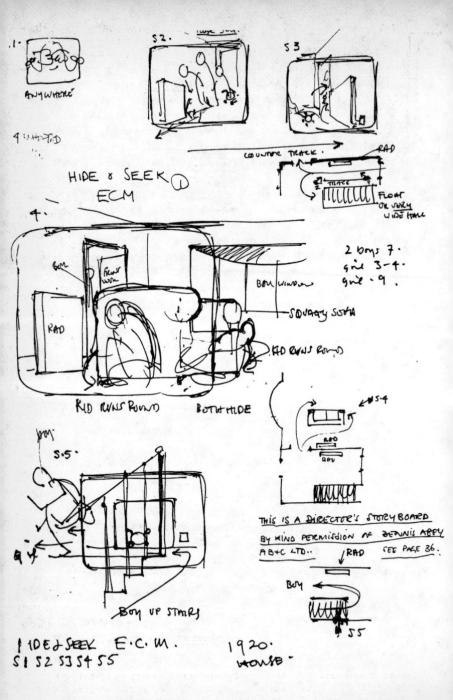

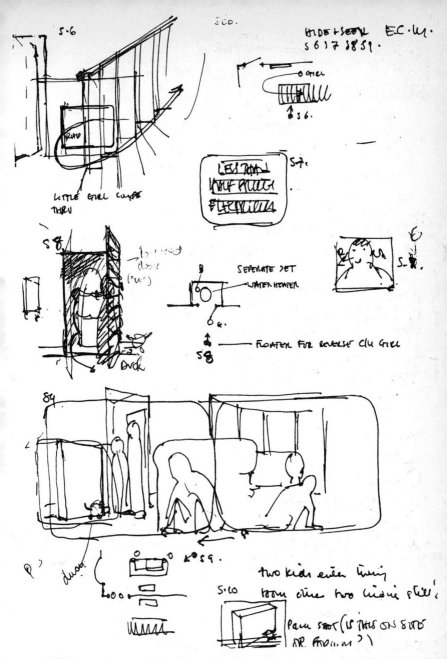

This is a director's "storyboard", with action implicit or indicated, sometimes outside the limits of the frame; shots, angles, movement, set-ups. A kind of near-moving picture sketchbook, a blue-print of the Director's based on the writer's script or scenario. Director: Dennis Abey, A.B.&C. Agency: Ted Bates. Creatives: Roger Musgrave, Bill Wood.

9

Selling Yourself

Now that you've learned how to go about writing the kind of TV commercial that can bring you fame, fortune, and the admiration of all those dear to you, you've got to find an outlet for that talent.

But that should be easier for you than most beginners.

What I've told you and what you've read puts you ahead of the game. You're one of the first to be told the secret of the magic shape. You've been told what makes a commercial effective. You know what a commercial should have if it's going to bring you awards. You know what to expect when your commercial is produced.

In other words, you have the unique experience of being led along the paths of real professionalism in the creation of TV commercials without ever having set foot in an advertising agency.

Getting ahead of the game

There are men and women in the commercial writing business who don't know as much as you know already, and they've probably been in the business for 3, 4, maybe 5 years or more.

They haven't realised there is such a thing as the magic shape. They haven't realised the need for integrity. They wouldn't know a simple benefit unless it was *back-lit, front-lit, top-lit, soft-focus,* and *over-speed.* Perhaps not even then.

And they certainly don't worry about expressing their ideas simply and credibly.

Nor do they have the quality that no amount of studying can give and which you have by nature: a fresh, uncluttered attitude. A clean, clear, uncomplicated picture of the consumer – fresh as you are from the ranks yourself. A picture that you made sure you printed indelibly on your mind before you got as far as the end of the second chapter of this book. (If you haven't done that, do it now before it is too late!)

So you are that much ahead, and you – even with your non-experience – are real competition. They should be worried. They should read and learn and understand what you have learned and understood. But they won't. So there you are – clear of the field. And you're going to earn their kind of money and more. You're going to compete with them for the top jobs.

Getting a reel

Now, how are you going to go about it?

First, you practise all that I've preached to you.

Get that magic shape into your head. Get yourself a tape recorder. Choose a selection of products to practise on and write yourself a collection of *specimens*, a spoken reel of TV commercials in the form of scenarios.

Half a dozen should be all you need to demonstrate the skills you have acquired. But be honest now. Before you put those six on tape, put yourself into your consumer shoes and ask yourself: would you respond to your commercials if you saw them on the screen? Are they original in some respect? Would they be a delight to watch? Do they have a simple, credible promise? Are they written with that all-important awareness that they will be seen by real people who lead real lives – not just the kind of lives that too many TV writers would like to think they lead?

The answer has got to be "Yes!" before you put them on your reel. Six "Yesses!" and you are ready for the next step. Getting an interview.

Getting an interview

The recruitment agency Recruitment agencies in the main are primarily concerned with finding and placing experienced people. You have only to look at the ads in the trade magazines and you will see that this is so. Very few vacancies for absolute beginners are ever advertised. The "chicken and egg" syndrome – how do you get experience without having a job to get experience – works against you here as elsewhere. But that is not to say that you won't find an interested, helpful, and sympathetic ear. Make contact with a few recruitment agencies if only to let them know you exist and are looking. When you find a job, let them know about it; they'll appreciate the common courtesy of your call and, what's more important, you suddenly become a more interesting person to them for the future. A list of recruitment agencies is on p 119.

The advertised vacancy The back pages of the trade magazines – *Campaign, Creative Review, Direction* – are where you'll find the kind of job you'll be applying for in two or three years' time. Very few beginners or "improvers" are wanted. But that doesn't mean to say you shouldn't keep your eye on these pages; if they want more experienced writers, chances are they've picked up a piece of business. Who knows, they may need a person and a quarter. Get in touch (see below) and tell them why you're calling. If nothing else, you'll score a few points for trying.

For the same reason, keep an eye on the new acquisition items: new business means they need more people. Get in touch (see below).

The cold call Cold calling in person may seem to be full of initiative and self-confidence, but it will probably be a total waste of time and tube fare. Whatever impressions you have gathered, in the good agencies – the kind you want to get into – they are very busy people.

So, if you are going to cold call, do it by phone. If you have to use a call box, buy a phone card! But don't expect too much. The most you should expect – unless it really is your lucky day – is finding out from the switchboard operator the name of the creative director; she/he is the one you want to see. Then ask to be put through. A

93

secretary will answer. You ask to be put through, using the creative director's first name as well as his surname, and give your own name without being asked for it – as if you were an old friend and your call was expected. (Some people have been known to pretend that they are returning the creative director's call to them. . . .) If the secretary has read this, well, settle for leaving your name and gently, politely let it be understood that you assume that it will be mentioned that you called. "You will tell him/her I called, won't you?" And that you'll be writing in at a later date.

If the creative director actually comes through on the line, say you have a reel you would like to present to her (or him). . . .

The mail-out The creative director is who you want to see. Either the creative director or someone the creative director deputes to interview writers.

You can cold call, or respond to a situations vacant ad. . . . Or you can set about mailing the creative director of each of the agencies on your short list. (You can go through the cold phone call routine mentioned above to find out the names of the creative directors if you don't know who they are.)

Address the envelope by hand. Leave out his/her title. The secretary might think it personal enough to leave unopened. And he might think it personal enough to open right away.

Inside there's your letter. Preferably typed. All it says is who you are, what you are doing, what you want to do, that you have a reel you'd like to present to him, and that you'll call in a couple of days to arrange a meeting.

Allow time for him to receive the letter. Then phone him before he has time to answer it. Tell the secretary you have written to first-name-surname and that you are calling to arrange the – the, remember, not a – meeting. If you're lucky, the meeting may be arranged there and then. Fine. If you're not you may be told to hang on.

Either of two things then happens:

1 Secretary: "I'm sorry but Mr Surname says there are no vacancies at the moment but he'll keep your letter on file."

You: "Good. Then I'd better let you have a more complete CV.

I'll put that in the post today. Thanks, very much – er – I'm sorry I didn't get your name."

Secretary: "Julia. Julia Surname."

You: "Well, thanks for your time, Julia. Bye."

2   Secretary: "I'm putting you through."

CD: "Hello."

You: "Hello. First-name-Surname? My name is first-name-Surname, and I think you ought to have got my letter by now."

CD: "Letter?"

You: "Oh, in that case I'll explain who I am and why I'm calling. . . ."

Any telephone salesperson will tell you the strategems behind all that chat. Suffice to say that, whatever the outcome of the telephone call, you now have an excuse/opportunity/reason to write again to the creative director. Say why you are writing again (to enclose your full CV) and, while you were at it, you thought you'd enclose a three-minute tape of your work. You'd appreciate any comments, dictated on the end of the tape.

Enclosed a stamped addressed Jiffy envelope; it's worth it if you've got this far. . . .

Then you wait a week longer than flesh and blood can be expected to wait – ie ten days – and you phone again. Whatever the result of this call, always, always finish off with the statement that you will be in touch again. Who knows, maybe you won't have to call them again. They might call you first. . . !

Your first interview

First of all, let me tell you about the man (probably) or the woman (possibly) you will meet when you have your first interview with a creative director.

Creative directors come in all shapes and sizes. Some are big and bluff and honest, he maintains. Others thin and intellectually brilliant, they think. Others are small and poisonous and egotistical. But you won't be meeting any of this kind, because you will have selected the kind of agency that you would like to work for, the kind of agency that does the kind of work you like and would like to do. This kind of agency has nothing to prove. It is rated within the industry and usually the creative director is the kind of person who has nothing to prove either. He's not in the business of impressing you. You are in the business of impressing him.

Now, which of your qualities do you bring to the fore?

Without knowing you personally it is difficult to advise; but there are certain ground rules it is worth learning.

1   Don't go to any agency that you wouldn't be proud to work for. I know that the pressures may be there to take a job at any cost. Don't. Or the next thing you know is you'll be trying to leave. And that's not fair on the people who hired you. And it's not good tactics for your career or for your self-esteem. You'll find yourself bad-mouthing the agency that gave you your first chance in order to impress someone at one of the agencies you'd like to work for. Sometimes it works. If it does then it's not the kind of agency I'd like you to work for.

2   If you do find yourself offered a job at an agency that wasn't in your top twenty, and if you do take it – then take it with the intention of learning everything that agency can teach you, whatever it is. Every agency – like every product – has a reason for existing. It can teach you something you didn't know. And once you've learned all you can from that particular agency, then that is the time to start looking around. And when you go for your next interview, stress what you've learned – not how they didn't understand you or couldn't accommodate your great inchoate talent. A good creative director will respect your honest intentions but not your dishonest ones. Even creative directors, for all their sins, have a sense of right and wrong: they may not be able to exercise it in their own lives but they appreciate it when they see others exercising it a little in theirs.

3   If the creative director offers criticism of your work, take it. Listen. He or she may say exactly the opposite to what the last or

the next creative director says, but then that's to be expected. You'll get six different opinions from six different people. Don't be confused, irritated, or obstreperous about it. Just listen. Take it in and try to see what they are getting at. Remember, you are a beginner. Play the beginner, if you have to. You may have sprung fully fledged from the egg; that's too bad. You just listen. You are the one who wants a job, not the creative director. And he wants someone he thinks can take creative direction until such time as they don't need it. And that time is a little beyond next Monday. If he's the creative director of the agency you want to work for, then the chances are he will recognise your precocious, fully-formed talent. And then maybe he won't. So you show you're ready to learn. Show you have the wit and the willingness – and you're well on the way to being an example of that raw talent that creative directors are proud to have discovered and "trained".

What are my chances?

This book was written for those among the flood of aspirants who are serious about making a career in advertising; for those among the many I have met, either as a creative director or lecturer, who have got what it takes but don't know how to present it; for those valuable people the industry might lose for want of a little fore-knowledge on how to get in.

I hope this and other books on other aspects of creative work will increase their chances.

And what are your chances? As good as you make them. And that requires of you that you learn as much about the business as you possibly can. Learn the language, for a start; there is a glossary of all italicised words at the end of this book.

Do your homework in front of your television screen.

Do your homework on the agencies you want to get into.

Use the precepts in this book to become skilled at putting a TV commercial together.

And practise, practise, and practise the craft until you realise that the work you did last month was rubbish by comparison with the work that you did last night.

Practise what you are going to say at your interview. Don't stumble through more than three without going home and working out where you did well or where you went wrong. Don't forget, it's potential as well as enthusiasm that creative directors take a chance on.

And finally, if you want to get in, don't give up. It is an inescapable fact: those who do give up never get in.

Summary

*   *Get together a "reel" of scenarios.*

*   *Get yourself a phone card and start cold calling.*

*   *Read the trade press intelligently: read the news, not just the ads.*

*   *By all means go for those agencies where you'd like to work, but if you end up somewhere else, remember: every agency has something to teach you.*

*   *Those who give up never get in.*

10

Planning Your Career

There's a bit at the beginning of *Winnie-the-Pooh* that describes Edward Bear coming downstairs – bumpety-bumpety-bump on the back of his head – dragged by Christopher Robin. And Edward thinks to himself that there must be a better way of coming downstairs than this but before he's had time to think of one, he's at the bottom.

It's all too easy, in any chosen work, to end up finding that Pooh-bear's concussive experience is an accurate metaphor for your career.

In your work as a TV commercial writer in advertising, you'll be so busy doing what you are doing that you have no time to stop and think: am I going about this career of mine in the right way? The times will come, as in any field of work, when you'll say to yourself that there must be a better way of earning a living. But, if you are anything like this writer, you'll never think too seriously about finding an alternative – in spite of the bumps and the knocks and the Christopher Robins – because there is no other way that gives you the fun, the challenge, the satisfaction, the association with intelligent, aware, stimulating people, the feeling of intellectual and creative superiority, and the rewards – except being a hyperactive professional billionaire.

There are, however, a few observations that I feel should be made at this point to help prevent your career being quite so mindlessly traumatic as Edward's descent; a few thoughts that will help you towards creating a solidly satisfying and rewarding career, rather than mindlessly using any and every seductive opportunity as a stepping stone to just another lily pad.

Perhaps the most significant decision you will find yourself making is whether you want to work for yourself within an agency all your life, or work for yourself outside an agency, or own your own agency eventually. The decision you make will not be decided by anything said here. It will be made by the kind of person you are: whether you are someone who works best in an organisation, or someone who is a born, go-it-alone, entrepreneur. I suspect that you may have made that decision already.

Whatever the decision, the common experience of everyone will be two, three, or four years – perhaps longer – working in an agency, and it is to this experience that we address ourselves here.

Stay a writer always

The best advice on planning your career was given in earlier chapters: find out what kind of commercial you are best at writing, find an agency that does the kind of work you like, and stay there for as long as the agency remains the kind of agency you want to work for and as long as you can succeed at writing the kind of commercial you are good at. The moment any of these factors change, the moment you recognise the need to write a different kind of commercial, or work in a different kind of agency, then – but only then – start looking around to see where those conditions can be satisfied.

That, of course, is too simple. If you are any good, you will be offered alternatives to doing what you like doing best. And this is real career-decision time.

Let me explain.

The advertising agency where you work is as hierarchical as the civil service. There are grades of people, grades of titles you've never heard of!

Junior writer

Senior writer

Group head

Copy chief

Copy director

Deputy creative director

Creative Director

Executive creative director

And even agencies where the creative director is also the Chairman

So there are dizzy heights to be descended.

And with each step in the hierarchy, the further you will go from doing what you like doing best: copywriting.

The decision will have to be made. Do you accept promotion that makes you responsible for other people and their work, or do you concentrate your time and creative talent on making your work better, unfettered by the demands of others?

Unfortunately, promotion is always made more seductive by the promise of more pay. Fortunately, more and more agencies are now wise enough to pay their creative people more money to go on doing what they do best, instead of paying them more money to start doing something they do less well: being a great copywriter doesn't always mean you'll be a great creative director.

The decision, nevertheless, will have to be made. If it is to take the promotion, I believe it is generally agreed that it is always wise – no matter what kind of promotion you take, no matter to what dizzy heights you find yourself called – never, never lose touch with your craft! That is what made you. It is your touchstone. Keep in touch with it. No matter how small the account you take under your wing as a copywriter, no matter how irksome and time-consuming your chairman's duties, always find time to practise your craft, even if it means slipping away for an hour or two from celebrating your USM launch or the raucous entertainment of the country house party you are throwing for your most important client. Once a writer, stay a writer. Then you'll always be able to have your say on equal footing with those 9-to-5, five days a week, unbelievably exorbitantly paid wretches who have decided to stay downstairs and have a hell of a time on the *creative floor*; and who, more than incidentally, are keeping your business in business.

Career or job sequence?

What other part of your career planning is more important than making sure you are being paid what you are worth?

The cynical answer is, there isn't one. But it's not the answer you will get from me.

I enjoyed what I was doing as a young writer so much that I was amazed that they actually paid me as well! I hope you experience the same amazement, but I also realize that money is harder to come by and it buys less than it used to, and so it is relatively more important. So here are a few observations on money.

Getting in is more important than what you get.

Once upon a time, a creative writer in advertising was paid exceptionally well compared with most other specialist jobs in and out of advertising. Then the disparity began to disappear in the early 1980s. But now, again comparatively, advertising salaries in general appear to be rising again, the creative person's salary rising no faster than the rest; there are exceptions, of course, and these are extraordinary and find great press and public interest!

But the question you want answered is: what are you worth?

The answer to that is: it varies according to when the question is asked, and it is impossible to quote here a figure that would be meaningful throughout what I hope will be the life of this book. But the answer can be found by close questioning of people you meet in the business, especially the people who are in a position to hire people or in the position of finding people jobs. One thing always seems clear: the starting salary varies very little from agency to agency; without conscious price-fixing, the figure seems to be arrived at by everyone by a kind of osmosis. Whatever it is, it will be more than a trainee nurse or a trainee teacher.

Your market value is always greater to someone else Once you have the experience, even as little as one or two years, moving about from agency to agency is the fastest way to push up your salary. Your value in the market outside is always greater than it is inside the agency. However, the move just for money is no move at all – and can only be justified by an increase of at least 30% or more. Even then it is wise to examine your motives: are you moving for money, or are you moving to extend yourself, to work with better people, to work on better accounts? Would you make the same move for the same money or even less? Are you moving *to* an agency, or are you just moving *away* from an agency; is the new job just an escape route, or a new trail to blaze?

Moral: never move for a better salary; always move for a better job that demands a better salary.

You are worth exactly what you can get There is no Burnham Scale in advertising. There is no union rate-for-the-job for writers. As a writer you are in there on your own – and that's the way most creative people like it. And that is why salaries can vary so much, why one writer of a given status, experience, and talent can command a bigger salary than another writer.

That is why salaries *can* vary, but why *do* they vary?

The answer is simply that one writer is an effective writer and the other is not. Effective writers, you see, are worth more than ineffective writers. Both kinds may put in the same amount of work/time/effort, but one makes his work stick. His work, his commercials, actually gets to be shown.

The ineffective writer complains about the restrictions placed upon his creative talent; too little time, too little money in the budget, too little to say, the product needs to be changed, the client won't appreciate good work when he sees it.

Meanwhile, the effective writer recognizes the amazing fact that: it is out of restrictions upon his freedom that come the best ideas. A tight budget, a bare-bones brief, restricted time – like a sentence of hanging, they all concentrate the mind wonderfully. They define the problem, they give you something to lean against, they give you something to respond to in a way that turns the challenge of restriction into a stimulus to creativity. The Pontin's commercial is a perfect example (page 64). All the constraints that a creative has nightmares about, but out of it came a campaign of five commercials for what other clients would pay for one – but each of those five will have won an award and done its job as a selling tool by the time this book is published. Beautifully simple commercials that have the structure, the integrity, and the simply-stated benefit that all great commercials have.

Effective writers complain less about the client, too. They know from experience that there isn't a client, be he ever so "non-creative", who doesn't recognize a great idea, a great commercial, in spite of himself. If it really is a great idea, and if you have presented it properly, then there's no client on earth that can resist it.

Great ideas are irresistible.

Summary

* *Never give up, or you'll never get in.*

* *Choose your list of agencies carefully.*

* *Move to a better job, not just to a better salary.*

* *Be effective, especially at presentations. Rehearse.*

* *A good idea is the hardest to find and the easiest to buy.*

* *Keep writing.*

Last Word

As you would expect, the ideas in this book and the advice given are based upon this writer's experience as a writer and creative director. Ask six other writers or creative directors and you would get different ideas, different advice, and different examples. But they haven't written this book.

It remains only to wish you luck in your chosen career, whether you stay a writer or simply use the unique experience, as so many have done, to go on to different things.

Good luck!

Glossary of Terms

In the writing and making of TV commercials and in the everyday life of advertising folk, there is a language used that sometimes confounds the lay-person. Here the most common usages are listed and explained. Argot, it may be; but jargon designed to keep secret, obscure, and protect, it is not.

First Words

Creatives: The latest label for those writers, art directors, and typographers whose job it is to think up and execute advertising ideas for the clients of the advertising agency.

Chapter 1

Creative department: The department where creatives live and where most of the very best ideas for ads and commercials regularly come from. Other departments can have good ideas, but not so dependably; and they don't quite have the expertise to know what to do with them when they get them.

Press ads: Advertisements that appear in the newspapers, magazines.

Brochures: Booklets prepared to give you more information about the product or service that the press ads have made you interested in.

Posters: Posters are outdoor advertising. Some are small, some big, some very big. And some have real cars stuck to them to demonstrate the sticking power of a particular brand of glue. Posters are famous for making creatives famous too.

Radio commercials: The commercials without pictures you hear on the independent radio stations between the programmes. A vastly under-exploited medium, wrongly used as a cheap substitute for TV. Listen to them. Learn to write them.

Creative director: He directs creatives, inspires by example, and creates the right atmosphere in which good ideas seed and flourish. (The horticultural metaphor is not an uncommon one in the advertising agency.)

Client: He pays for the broadcasting of all those great ideas the creatives get.

Account executives: Not money men in the sense of Accounts departments, but money men nevertheless in that they are largely responsible for the profitable operation of the clients' business they administer in the agency. They also know about marketing, research, media, copywriting, TV production, print processes, layout, good taste, good wine, good food. Just the way creatives do.

Target audience: The people out there who are in a position, financially, socially, morally, to buy what you are writing a commercial about.

C^1C^2: A socio-demographical section of the total population. Somewhere below the comfortably-off lower middle classes, I'd say. But find out for yourself; things change so quickly.

George and Lynn: A strip cartoon couple regularly appearing in the *Sun.* Read it regularly for more than the obvious reason. It says something about the aspirations of the *Sun*'s readership – the *Sun* doesn't get it wrong.

Pitchman: The chap inside your TV set who shouts at you over what could possibly be, visually, a very well-made commercial.

Chapter 2

TV production company: A company that specialises in turning your script into a film.

Slice of life: A term used to describe a commercial that purports to show real people in real life. It used to be applied to a commercial with something of a sneer, until it was replaced by drama-real (see page 27).

Supers: The words you see printed up on the screen over the picture.

In-studio: A film shoot that takes place indoors as opposed to on a beach in the Bahamas.

Animation: When things that have no possible life of their own seem to be alive. Milk bottles talk. Simple black lines look and move like imitation people. Yoghurt cartons manifest themselves from nowhere: that's animation.

Stop motion: Usually a technique employed in animation; the camera is stopped every few seconds so that changes can be made to the subject being filmed. When the film is run continuously, what you see looks like magic.

Stepped frames: Individual frames in the length of film are repeated by a laboratory process; the effect is to extend the moment of action. Films of the Great War are treated this way so that our viewing of that tragic mistake makes it look less of a farce.

Over-cranking: Deliberately running the camera at higher speeds so that the effect when seen is slow-motion. Shampoo commercials use it!

Under-cranking: The opposite to the above.

Artwork: Titles, supers (see above), photographed usually by a rostrum camera (see below).

Spokesman: Old-fashioned word for the man presenting the product to you.

Rostrum camera: A film camera secured directly over a flat bed to photograph artwork.

Film footage: The film run through the camera, usually separated into "takes" and "scenes" shown on that clapper-board we are all familiar with.

Chapter Three

Presentation: A formal or informal presenting of creative work to whomsoever has to approve it, at whatever stage it has reached.

Script: Your idea put down on paper in two columns, left-hand for what you will see, right-hand for what you will hear.

Storyboard: A sometimes larger than necessary piece of board on which the "story" of your commercial is depicted.

Sound effects: Bees buzzing, doors slamming, tyres screeching. . . .

Art director: Not to be confused with the art director from the agency. This art director designs the set and selects everything on it except the actors.

Frames: 1 The pictures on a storyboard; 2 The individual exposures in a length of film.

Pre-production meeting: The meeting at which the people directly responsible for the making of the commercial gather and prepare for the Production meeting.

Scenario: A narrative description of the commercial.

Cinematically: As if you were describing a moving film, not words and static pictures.

Chapter Four

Media department: The department of an advertising agency that specialises in deciding where the client's media money should be spent: in newspapers, on TV, on radio, on posters, on direct marketing, on all or on some in any combination.

Studio floor: Where they make the commercial.

Editor's cutting rooms: Where you go to view a collage of film footage taken from selected "takes". Sometimes the most creative part of the process and a real life-saver!

Non-creative people: Those not actually paid to come up with ideas for commercials.

Chapter Five

Award winning commercial: More often an admiring description of a commercial or a prophesy than a statement of fact.

Chapter Six

Product category: The kind of product – soap-powder, perfume, computer, etc....

USP: Unique Selling Proposition, that apparently unique quality about the product which, when expressed (usually in words, rarely in pictures), has the power of selling the product to the potential buyer in the face of all competition.

Chapter Seven

Marketing strategy: How the product will be sold in the widest sense, which usually includes methods of distribution, pricing, and packaging, as well as advertising.

Advertising strategy: How the product will be advertised in the widest sense. Big budget, small budget, print or TV, direct marketing.

Copy strategy: How the product will be presented to the consumer, what kind of product it will be; rather like choosing a career for your children.

Product attributes: What the product has going for it in physical or image terms.

Rough cut: A rough assembling of selected footage, just to see whether it is going to work as a film. Not the finished film, remember.

Production values: All those brilliant artifices of lighting, set design, camera work that you will never be able to write into your commercial but which the director and the production company are absolutely brilliant at putting in and which sometimes save a weak idea.

Film director: The person who directs the shooting of your script.

Chapter Eight

Production: The whole process of planning, shooting, editing, and finishing the making of your script into a film.

Producer: The man or woman in the agency responsible for the administration and logistics of making the film, and for its final technical quality.

Director's reels: A collection of commercials directed by a director and carried about in a silver can as big as a soup plate by the production company producer or his lad.

Voice-over: The voice you hear around the edges of the commercial you are watching: the unseen narrator.

Graduate trainees: The product of the agency world's annual gathering from the crop of university and polytechnic graduates.

Shot: Past tense of the verb, meaning here to photograph with a cine-camera.

Pre-production: All the things that have to be done so that the commercial will actually get made on the day.

Production unit: The collection of film people brought together to make your commercial.

Camera crew: The smaller unit within the production unit who are responsible for operating the camera, keeping the picture in focus, pushing and pulling the camera (when necessary); formation swimming has nothing on their precision team-work.

Art director: This art director (as distinct from the agency art director) designs and supervises the construction of the film set.

Lighting: Refers either to the effect of the lighting of the set or, strange as it may seem, the person who controls the lighting of the scene.

Props: The objects of all kinds that are essential to the action or the appearance of the film; also applied to the person who is responsible for these objects.

Casting director: The person who knows who to put on the list of possible candidates for the signal honour of working in your commercial.

Actors: The people (and the animals) appearing in your commercial.

Studio: The place where your commercial is made.

Transport: The big vans carrying the film equipment and the limos carrying the clients to and from the shoot. The latter arrive much later than the former.

Catering: Whoever it is who provides those wonderful bacon rolls in the morning, lunch at lunchtime, and terrible sticky buns at teatime, usually cooked and served from a post-war ex-Green Line coach.

Quote: An estimate, for agency and client approval, prepared by the production company.

Editing suites: Posh cutting rooms, usually with some projection facility.

Editors: The people who make sense out of the hundreds of feet of film footage, reducing it down to a marvellously coherent 30 seconds.

Projection room: Usually a small viewing theatre where you can watch reels of film shot by directors you are thinking of using.

Present: To present a script is to "enact" it for the benefit of some significant other person.

Call sheet: This is where you may see your name if they like you or your work, but well down the list, below important people like the camera man, props man, client, etc.

Rushes: Overnight prints of the film shot the day before, looked at not for quality but to see whether you can start breathing again.

Takes: Film footage shot of any part of any given sequence in the commercial.

Footage: The film shot.

Printed: Takes selected by the director, processed so that prints for projection and viewing can be made.

Editing: The very skilled mystery and craft of putting together selected takes to produce the desired sequence of action.

Director's cut: His idea of how the commercial should look if he were making a film.

Post-production: The many processes through which the shot film is taken before it finally becomes the finished film.

Fine-cutting: One of the last stages of preparing the finished film, usually a matter of a frame here and a frame there. This is really where you leave it to your editor and trust him.

Sound track: All the sounds you hear while you are watching the commercial.

Sound studio: Where sound tracks are recorded.

Sound engineer: The person who pushes up and pulls down as many as 24 different sliding controls on a control panel in order to get just the right mix and balance of sounds when the sound track is being recorded.

Recording session: The time you spend enjoying yourself in a sound studio listening to the sound track being recorded.

Voice artist: A person who reads or sings what you have written and does it so effortlessly and artlessly that you think it's too easy – until you try doing it yourself.

Shooting plan: Director's working "storyboard".

Chapter Nine

Back-lit, front-lit, top-lit: Positions of main lighting designed to flatter the subject.

Soft focus: If you wear glasses, take them off: that's soft focus.

Over-speed: Over-cranking.

Specimens: Examples of your work.

Chapter Ten

Creative floor: The creative department of an agency, usually set well apart from the rest.

Bibliography

TV copywriting won't be the only thing you are expected to do in an advertising agency. You need to know how to write press ads, posters, brochures, and leaflets. You need to know a little of the marketing context in which you will be expected to operate. You will also need to be exposed to other points of view than mine, and to know what kind of people you are working with and how to work with them. The following titles will help.

William Goldman, *Adventures in the Screen Trade,* Macdonald, 1984

Rosser Reeves, *Reality in Advertising,* Alfred A. Knopf, New York, 1977

David Ogilvy, *Ogilvy on Advertising,* Pan, 1983
Winston Fletcher, *Commercial breaks,* Advertising Press, London, 1984

British Design & Art Direction, Internos Books, London (Annual)
A A Milne, *Winnie-the-Pooh*, Methuen, London

Alastair Crompton, *The Craft of Copywriting,* Century Hutchinson, London, 2nd edn, 1987

College Courses In Advertising

The number of colleges offering courses in the practise of any aspect of work in the advertising world are few. The longest-established seem to be the best, although one immensely impressive school has opened in the last couple of years in London. Thankfully, Principals and course tutors now realise that graphics and fine art are not quite all that is expected of you in the day to day practise of the craft of advertising, and are preparing courses that involve practising advertising men in the teaching of their particular skills. Here is but a short list of colleges with which I have had some dealings, or have been recommended to me.

Amersham College, Stanley Hill, Amersham, Bucks., HP7 9HN.

Bristol Polytechnic, Coldharbour Lane, Frenchay, Bristol, BS16 1QY.

Kingston Polytechnic, Millenium House, 21 Eden Walk, Kingston upon Thames, KT1 1BL.

Hounslow Borough College, London Rd., Isleworth, Middx., TW7 4HS.

Manchester Polytechnic, All Saints Building, Oxford Road, Manchester, Lancs.

Newcastle College of Arts and Technology, Rye Hill, Newcastle-upon-Tyne.

School of Communication Arts, Woodbridge House, 9 Haywards Place, London, E.C.1.

Watford College, Hempstead Road, Watford, WD1 3EZ.

Further reference: Directory of Further Education, published by
Hobsons Ltd., Bateman Street, Cambridge.

Recruitment Agencies

Employment agencies need to be licenced by government and one condition of their being licenced is that they do not charge a fee to the people they place.* In other words, you are not required to pay anyone anything to find you a job.

The employment agency is paid a fee by the employer or company for whom it is acting; the fee represents the sometimes enormous amount of time and effort spent on searching for and deciding upon the right person for the job; some employment agencies – who are to be praised – invest a considerable amount of time and concern on behalf of students and juniors, even though these are not the most profitable clients.

The author has spoken to all the recruitment agencies listed below. I thank them for their support and hope that they, in turn, receive the support they deserve from the advertising industry as a whole.

Creative Selection, 189 Regent Street, London W1R 7WD
Joyce McMillan & Partners, 10/6 Stirling Court, Marshall Street, London W1V 1LQ
Star Writers & Art Directors, 82 Old Brompton Road, London SW7 3LQ
The Creative Centre, 42 Maiden Lane, London WC2E 7LJ
The People Business (Midlands) Ltd, 46a Castle Street, Hinckley, Leicester LE10 1DD

*except to performers and certain other workers in the entertainment field, and to photographic or fashion models (The Employment Agencies Act, 1973, DoE publication PL 594 (4th rev))

The Talent Store, 11 Eccleston St, London SW1W 9LX
The Workhouse, 75 New Bond Street, London W1Y 9DD
Young People in Advertising, 4 John Spencer Square, Canonbury,
London N1 2LZ

INDEX

Account executive, 11, 108
Advertising
  agency, 10
  strategy, 67
Animation, 29, 30, 109
Art Director, 34, 80, 113
Artwork, 29, 110
Arts
  visual, 26
  and culture, 22
Apple computers, 28
Audience, target, 13, 108
Awards, 53-56, 111

Benefit, 58-61
Book at Bedtime, 36
Brief, creative, 80, 81, 103
British Film Industry, 27, 55
Brochures, 107
Budget, advertising, 65

Camera
  work, 27
  crew, 77, 113
Career planning, 99-104
Cartoon, 29-31
Catering, 77, 114
Chord,
  music, 44-48

major, 44
Christopher Robin, 99
Classification, C^1 C^2, 15-16, 108
Client, 11, 24, 49, 87, 108
Cold calling, 93
Commercials, 7-8
  award-winning, 53, 56
  great, 57-58
  making your, 75-89
Cointreau, 27
Creative, 8, 10, 107
Creative Director, 11, 94-97,
  108
Creative floor/department, 10,
  107, 116
Creative Handbook, 77
Creativity, 21-22, 26
Cutting room, 83
CV, 95

Delight, quality of, 14
Demonstration, 28
Director, Film, 48, 82-87
  choice of, 78, 81-82, 85-86,
  113
Director's cut, 83, 115
Director's reel, 113
Director's shooting plan, 86,
  116

Drama
  - doc, 27
  - real, 27

Editing, 83, 115
  rough cut, 71, 83, 112
  suite, 78, 114
Editor, 78, 83, 114
Editor's cutting rooms, 83, 111
Education, 17
Edward Bear, 99
Entertainment value, 13-15
Eric Clucas & Associates, 13-14

Famous people, 28
Fantasy, 18
Fourth idea, 11

George and Lynn, 16, 108
Great commercial! 57-63
Group discussion, 31

Humour, 14

Ideas, 22-27, 31
Integrity, in commercials, 54, 57-59
Interview, 93
Instinct, 14-16

John Cleese, 15

Kirkwood, R.H., 13
Kirkwood Company, The, 13

Length,
  writing to, 45
  voice over test of, 48
Leverhulme, Lord, 65
Live action, 29

Magic Shape, The, 41-51

Mail-out, 94
Market value, a writer's, 102-103
Marketing strategy, 67
Media,
  personality, 27
  department, 42, 111
Midland Bank, 28
Monty Python's Flying Circus, 29
Music
  director, 25
  jingle, 46
  music-lovers, 46
  track, 85
Musicians, 46, 85
Musicologists, 46

Non-creative people, 49

O, The Big, 42-44
Outsiders, 9

Pitchman, 17, 109
Pontins, 103
Posters, 108
Post-production
  fine-cut, 84, 115
  rough-cut, 71, 83
  rushes, 83
Press ads., 107
Pilkington Glass, 28
Presentation, 33, 110
  of scenarios, 34-38, 79
  script/storyboard, 33-34, 41
  to Director, 79
Pre-production
  meeting, 80, 111, 113
  set design, 80
  casting, 80
  wardrobe, 81
  product, 81

THE CRAFT
OF TV COPYWRITING

John Harding

Allison & Busby
Published by W.H. Allen & Co. Plc

props, 114
Producer, TV, 75, 113
Product
  attributes, 68, 112
  category, 61, 112
  ideas, 23-25
Production
  commercial, 75, 113
  values, 71, 112
  role of writer in, 76
  company, 27, 77, 78, 109
  company producer, 78
  unit, 77
  pre-production meeting, 80,
    111
  post-production, 83
Props, 114

Quality of life, 18

Radio commercials, 108
Reality in advertising, 18-19,
  24, 54, 60, 62, 117
Recording session, 84, 116
Recruitment agencies, 119
Research, 65-73
  ideas from, 31
  Product, 31
  Consumer, 31
  Group discussions, 31, 69, 71
Reels, director's, sample, 27, 92
Rolls Royce, 23
Romance, 18
Rosser Reeves, 62, 117

Salaries for beginners, 102
Satire, 19
Saatchi & Saatchi, 72
Scenario,
  for research, 72
  use in presentations, 34-38,
    79

Script, 33-34, 110
  and storyboard, 33-34, 41,
    110
  for research, 71
Sound
  effect, 34, 36, 110
  engineer, 84, 116
  music track, 85
  studio, 84, 115
  track, 84, 115
Specimens/samples, writers',
  92, 116
Storyboard
  frames, 34, 111
  script and, 33-34, 41, 110
Strategy
  Marketing, 67, 112
  Advertising, 67, 112
  Copy, 67, 112
Studio floor, 114
Supers, 109
Surreal, 29, 60

Talking heads, 17
Target audience, 13, 108
Testimonial, 28-29
The third ingredient, 58-59
Tony Brignull, 21

Unique Selling Proposition
  (U.S.P.), 60-63

Voice over/artist, 84, 113, 116
Volkswagen, 23

Winston Fletcher, 14, 117
Writer
  creative, 14, 15
  effective, 103
  kinds of, 17-18
  role of, 76